A Kick
in the
Assets

Also by Tod Barnhart

The Five Rituals of Wealth

10

Take-Charge Strategies for Building the Wealth You Want

A Kick
in the
Assets

Tod Barnhart

G. P. Putnam's Sons
New York

G. P. Putnam's Sons
Publishers Since 1838
a member of
Penguin Putnam Inc.
375 Hudson Street
New York, NY 10014

This book is sold with the understanding that neither the author nor the publisher is engaged in rendering legal, accounting, or financial services. As each financial situation is unique, questions relevant to the practice of law, accounting, or personal finance and specific to the individual should be addressed to an appropriate professional for proper evaluation and advice.

The author and publisher specifically disclaim any liability, loss, or risk, personal or otherwise, which is incurred as a consequence, directly or indirectly, of the use and application of any of the contents of this work.

Library of Congress Cataloging-in-Publication Data

Barnhart, Tod, date.
    A kick in the assets: ten take-charge strategies for building the
    wealth you want / Tod Barnhart.
        p.   cm.
    Includes index.
    ISBN 0-399-14430-7
    1. Finance, Personal.   2. Investments.   I. Title.
    HG179.B334   1998   98-20424 CIP
    332.024'01—dc21

Printed in the United States of America

10 9 8 7 6 5 4 3 2 1

This book is printed on acid-free paper. ∞

BOOK DESIGN BY JUDITH STAGNITTO ABBATE

Dedicated to the mystery and the journey.
I'm just hangin' on for the ride.

ACKNOWLEDGMENTS

Writing a book is not an easy process. It's tough work for a guy like me who doesn't sit still very well.

However, the path a work like this has to take before you come to hold it in your hot little hands is even more difficult. An agent has to believe in it. A publisher has to believe in it. Publicity and media people have to believe in it. The bookstores have to believe in it. And finally, you, the reader, must absolutely believe—enough to make a purchase and invest your reading time.

So, the first person I would like to thank is YOU—for believing in this book enough to commit yourself. No writer survives unless his readers believe. You may not know it, but you're now and forever on the team.

As the author, I'm going to get enough credit for this thing. My name's on the front. But you've probably not had a chance to get to know or thank the other hardworking people on our team. So read the following acknowledgments, if you will, with an appreciative thought in your heart for our "teammates behind the scenes" who've made *A Kick in the Assets* a dream come true.

Let's thank:

Jan Miller, our literary agent. You are in a class by yourself, Jan. Love your guts! *And* her support staff, Lisa, Elizabeth, Shannon, and Joy. Thanks a ton.

Jeremy Katz, our super editor at Putnam. You're a major winner. The title, *A Kick in the Assets*, was just one of Jeremy's brainchildren. *Get the picture?*

Elizabeth Himelfarb at Putnam. Thanks for your hard work and effort on our behalf.

Cindy, my wonderful wife (OUR definitely does not apply. She's mine!). And she's the best. *Would you want to live with an author/writer/speaker/financier?*

Anthony Robbins, who continues to be the ultimate role model of possibility.

Jeff and Eric and TPN faculty and distributors, who send our TV message to the world.

Special thanks to my family and friends for their support and encouragement: Mom and Pop, Jim and Tricia, Dad and Karen, Paul and Marie, John and Traci, Jennifer, Mike, and Roberta, Linda and Bill, Ronnie and Kristy, Cliff and Tammy, Lani and Kenn, Sandy and Dave, Grandma Wanda, Granny Mullin, Hector and Faye, Bill and Debra, Jeff and Julie, LiftKit, Jeff Arch, Will Hasley, Don Connelly, Craig Meier, Kevin Waller, Dave and Renatta, Angie, David Alford, and The Fine Diners: Ellen, Andy, Jim, and Judy.

Contents

A Kick

in the

Assets

Dazed and Confused:
Financial Groundwork and Habits

Totally and royally outta control, Matt feathers the cat box with bills, bank statements, and lottery tickets.

Do not let the future be held hostage by the past.

—Neil Maxwell

■ 1: A KICK IN THE ASSETS

All men who have turned out worth anything have had a chief hand in their own education.

—**Sir Walter Scott**

Q: Who needs *A Kick in the Assets?*
A: I think we all do, but the real question is, "How hard and which boot?" Sure, we can all use some gentle encouragement from time to time, as we pass between the stages in our lives. But where's that shove going to come from, and where's it going to take you? You've already given this consideration, no doubt, because you've picked up this book.

So, congratulations. You've taken the first step. You've also probably realized a few other things:

1. You need money
2. Actually, you're quite addicted
3. You now have a real life, and
4. Money will kick your ass if you let it

You've also realized that it's time to gain control. Let me jump in by offering our first scenario; it involves our road-test couple, Matt and Jenny.

■ SCENARIO

Matt and Jenny lead a familiar life. They both work hard and have held jobs long enough to know that there's no free lunch. Lately, however, they've been looking into the future more and more and have decided that they want more out of life. They want their dreams to come true. They want to buy a home, travel the world, send their children to the best schools, and retire in luxury someday. Then reality sets in. They've been working for some time now, waiting for something to happen that will change their financial lives, but for them, it's always the same old script: too much month left at the end of the money, not enough time to do everything, and not enough energy to enjoy what little time and money they do have.

So, time for the real world:

1. Each of us is living out a script when it comes to money.
2. For the most part, we wrote that financial screenplay for ourselves.

All things considered, Matt and Jenny have an OK life. Still, they'd like to go to the next level. They'd like their financial screenplay to change. But what's the catalyst? What's going to propel Matt and Jenny into the financial life of their dreams?

What's going to change Matt and Jenny's financial screenplay? Matt and Jenny. That's what.

A Kick in the Assets is a wake-up call. It's the "swift kick" that helps us accept one major fact: good or bad, for the most part, our "screenplay" is the result of the choices we've made. Each of us, over time, creates our financial history from our actions, ideals, expectations, knowledge, and skill. We made it.

And we are the only ones who can change it.

Throughout this book, you'll acquire the knowledge you need to rewrite your screenplay, and this time, it will be action-packed, and the good guy will come out on top.

Don't you know the somebody who's perpetually in debt? Or a cheapskate? What about a miser? A spendthrift? A show-off? A martyr? A moocher?

When it comes to money we all have a role that feels comfortable, a story that fits.

So, *A Kick in the Assets* is the first step. It's the look in the financial mirror while asking yourself, "Do I really belong here? Or am I comfortable only because I've played this role before?"

Before we get rolling, let me remind you that there is no screenplay without any conflict. Each stage of the financial journey comes with its own set of challenges.

This book will lay it all out for you, step by step, on your way to living the life you dream about and building the wealth you want.

Enough talk. Let's get started.

First order of business is to cure the writer's block that's taking away your drive and keeping your financial screenplay in this rut.

What's Your Excuse?

"I've let things go so long it's hopeless. There's no way I can straighten
out this mess."

"The whole money system is stupid. The way it should be is . . ."

"I've always been lucky, so something will work out."

"I'm too young."

"I'm too old."

"I'm not doing *that* bad anyway."

"I'm too strapped for cash."

"I'll start next year, uh . . . when I get a raise. That's the ticket, yeah."

"What if I get my financial life together and then blow it because . . .
I always do anyway?"

"I'm too busy to keep track of my expenses."

"I can't be bothered with details; I'm an artist (or an architect, or
other important person)."

OK, I'll admit: **There are a million reasons for *not* achieving your
dreams.** And every single one of them will drag you under if you let it.

However, to succeed, it only takes **one powerful reason** why you're
going to DO IT; **one reason** why you're committed to kicking down the
damn wall and making wealth work for you. That **one reason,** however,
you'll have to uncover for yourself. That's the only way it has any power.

So? Well? You bought this book for *A Kick in the Assets*, right? Knock off
the whining and DO IT. And eat your vegetables. It's for your own good.

I know you're ready to roll, but before you jump in with your eager mind,
let me clarify a few things:

1. I've found success, but I don't know everything—not even close.
2. I've been beaten up by money, just like you.
3. I've studied much of the financial experts out there; and
4. They're confused too, at times. Money's a broad issue.

However, there's hope. Succeeding with money is a sort of game. With
rules you can learn. Which means: you absolutely, positively, can grow
wealthy.

It's doable. And you have the most powerful ally on your side: TIME.

I'm not kidding. Of the one hundred financial tools and strategies we're
going to discuss, TIME is the most valuable. If you're under forty-five and
considering retirement planning, you're gonna be HUGE. That's easy. You've

got time to let the tools work, perhaps make a few mistakes, recover, and still wind up richer than Midas.

Now, having announced that I'm no guru, here's what I have done:

1. Spent the last decade up-to-date and focused on wealth and money.
2. Rubbed shoulders with bright money minds (not actually touching the cerebrum).
3. Authored best-selling books and tapes, advised a bunch of rich folks, helped thousands of other people make it, hosted a TV money show, lectured a ton, done hundreds of radio and TV appearances, and ran my own advisory firm.
4. Spanked Jenny McCarthy (making sure you're listening . . .)
5. Worried too much over stupid, insignificant setbacks as if my life depended on it.

So, I've tried to get to the nuts and bolts with this book, talking about the worry-worthy stuff in detail, glazing over what I think is bubble gum, and definitely, definitely, giving you enough information to help you sidestep the scams and pitfalls I've encountered over the past ten years.

Oh, and the swift kick you were supposed to receive?

Stop cringing. It's over. You've given it to yourself. You've picked up this book and probably taken other steps in the right direction. You're ready. You've suffered enough.

Let's go.

2. DEFINE SUCCESS

It's too late. I've spent too many years doing exactly what was expected of me: being a good son, a good husband, a good father. In my company I'm known as a "good soldier." When I ask myself what I am about, I'd have to say I don't know anymore. I've tried for so long to fit in, I've held back for so long, I don't know what or who I am.
—**A middle-aged executive at a multinational corporation**

■ SCENARIO

Matt and Jenny are winners. They're both educated, hard-working, and they share an energetic zest for life. Lately, however, they feel as though they've lost a bit of focus. Oh sure, they meet expectations at work—quotas, deadlines, responsibilities—but still, they've gotten so caught up in the race of their daily lives that sometimes they've forgotten what they were after in the first place. With their bosses' expectations, their financial obligations, and the constant pressure to succeed, they've fallen into the rut of pleasing other people. They know what it takes to get the promotion, the new car, the "employee of the month" certificate, but is that all they really want out of life? Is that all they signed on for?

Here's the common drill: get out of school, take the highest-paying job offered, start dressing like your boss, jump through the hoops to gain some measure of respect, gain respect and promotions, get to be the boss, notice other people beginning to dress like you, impose hoops for them to jump through, change jobs because it's not progressing fast enough, set your sights on another rung, start dressing like that boss, jump through the hoops . . .

You get the picture.

Most of us started out with an ideal vision of what we wanted out of life. So, we committed ourselves, and we plugged away. But something happened: we "people-pleased" our way to the top and made some compromises along the way. We attended that conference in Atlanta to win the sales contest. We had to win the contest to get recognition enough to service that plum account. We had to service that plum account to get that bonus. The boss, in turn, heaped on more responsibility, which gave us a promotion, which took us to that training seminar in Las Vegas, which prepared us for the next promotion. And so on.

STOP. What's happened here?

Somewhere along the way, we lost our driving vision. We've fallen into somebody else's plan. We've jumped through their hoops and forgotten what we desired in the first place. What happened to seeing the world? Running that 10K? Times Square on New Year's Eve? How about that trip to Mexico we'd dreamed about?

To glide down the path to success, you've got to clearly envision what's waiting at the end. You get the point: if we don't hold firmly to our own vision, we're at substantial risk of falling into somebody else's plan. You already know that work pressure can alter your professional behavior enormously, but most people don't realize that its effect ripples through their whole life.

Q: What if your company's idea of success is different from your own?

What if your family/spouse's idea of success is different from your own?

What if you've forgotten what your own idea of success is?

Or never had a clue?

A: Rat race, treadmill, big-time burnout, unhappiness galore!

A bit extreme, I'll agree, but can you relate? **If you don't know what you want, you won't get it.** Worse, you may achieve success and not even know it. So, it's very simple: right here, right now, take a stand for what you want. Define success for yourself, and nobody else. Then you will have the tool to focus your life's vision.

"What are you talking about?" you ask.

To answer, let me introduce one of America's most notable historical figures, Ben Franklin.

No dummy, as you know, Ben Franklin had a code that he tried to live by, regardless of the requirements imposed upon his day. His "list of virtues" was his own way of remaining true to his personal idea of success every day. In the evenings, in his daily journal, he'd checkmark each virtue that a daily task had fulfilled. Here's his list; then I'll explain further.

Ben Franklin's Code of Thirteen Virtues

1. Temperance	**8.** Justice
2. Silence	**9.** Moderation
3. Order	**10.** Cleanliness
4. Resolution	**11.** Tranquillity
5. Frugality	**12.** Chastity
6. Industry	**13.** Humility
7. Sincerity	

Now, you may have noticed that "win sales contest" and "get promotion" were not on the list. His virtues were not things he tried to win or achieve. Instead, they were things he tried to *be*. And by *be*ing sincere and just and so on, he achieved success. Make sense?

Now let's design your own code of virtues. **Let it serve as your personal DEFINITION OF SUCCESS.** First, I'll share mine as an example:

Tod Barnhart's Code of Fourteen Virtues

1. Passion	**8.** Responsibility
2. Happiness	**9.** Appreciation
3. Radiance	**10.** Genuineness
4. Creativity	**11.** Proactiveness
5. Warmth	**12.** Confidence
6. Generosity	**13.** Uniqueness
7. Health	**14.** Empathy

Think about this: If every day you live by your code and make it a point to *be* everything on your list, you achieve your ideals. Every day. By your own definition, you have found success. And won't you feel so much more positive and alive when you measure yourself by the things that you have total control over, instead of the things that you don't? Won't that power help you increase your performance and income?

I think you know the answer. So raise me by one; each generation should improve upon the last! I challenge you to live by a code of fifteen virtues.

Pull out a notebook. Buy one special—your first investment. You'll need it to set goals and track progress and the like. It will be your new screenplay, chronicling your rewriting of your own financial life. So, please get the book and start writing. Go.

■ **EXERCISE:**

In your notebook, list Your Code of Fifteen Virtues. There is only one rule, and it is simple: **Each virtue must be totally within your control. It must be something you can be.**

Maybe I'm easily impressed, but I think Old Ben was a guy who kicked major butt: he was a successful writer, wealthy, influential in affairs of state, blah, blah, blah. I have a hard time believing that he would engage in an airy-fairy waste of time. The chastity thing is kind of lame, but the man wasn't perfect. So, if you didn't do the exercise, and you have even an ounce of respect for our august forefathers, go back and do it NOW. Pretty please.

Is that a reel of your old financial flick I see on the cutting-room floor?

To Do:

■ Buy your notebook.
■ Record your Code of Fifteen Virtues.

▪ 3. RAISE YOUR STANDARDS

When a fantasy turns you on, you're obligated to God and nature to start doing it—right away.

—Stewart Brand

▪ SCENARIO

Matt and Jenny are fun-loving people. Heck, last week Matt told a joke to his best customer. Just last year, they both went to Omaha for Thanksgiving with their families, and it's only been three (or four or five) years since their last major vacation. Oh, and Jenny goes to aerobics three times a week. That's fun, right? Matt's going to get back into softball, too—as soon as work dies down. Now that I'm writing it, it doesn't sound too good, but they really are an active, exciting couple. Wait, wait, wait, don't let me forget to mention—a-ha: Matt and Jenny both go to the movies at least twice a month. Not so bad for a coupla hardworking DINKS (Dual Income, No Kids—yet).

Most people don't achieve the financial success they deserve simply because **they have low standards.** Don't get me wrong. They say they want more money and more success, but it's just that they've settled into a lifestyle that they're somewhat comfortable with. And guess what? They always seem to have *just* enough money to support *that* lifestyle.

We all have some sort of internal idea of where we think we belong—an automatic thermostat, if you will. If something happens to throw off the balance, we turn up the heat: work more, ask for a raise, or change jobs. However, as long as we're not inconvenienced too dreadfully, we tend to mark time; we do what we've always done and get what we've always gotten. Oh, sure, we'd take that fat raise or cash that big check if it were thrown at us.

But guess what? Nobody just throws money at anybody. You have to earn it, demand it, expect it. So to break out of your financial screenplay, you have to raise your standards. What are you willing to settle for?

In the last section, you discovered what success means for you. Now, you will begin to see where your fifteen virtues might lead you. And the first step is to raise your financial standards. To do that, you must stretch your mind; push your vision to its outer limits. Your new, higher standard has to be clearly envisioned beforehand.

A powerful way to motivate yourself to raise your standards and have fun in the process is to start **habitually** dreaming like a kid again. This is not a frivolous exercise. It's the beginning of the goal-setting process, and the excitement of the exercise is enough to pull you toward your dreams. And notice I say "habitually." Stretching your vision and standards takes practice, but only practice will make them come alive. You can wish and want, but when it comes time to demand a raise or start that business, you'd better imagine it so clearly you can see it standing before you. Make sense?

■ EXERCISE:

So get your dreamer hat on and answer four powerful questions. Don't answer with what you think you should *say, or what you think* other people *would want to hear. Just answer them quietly, thoroughly, for yourself. Think about them, riff on them, and begin your fantasy life. Then, write the answer to each in your notebook. You'll want to refer to them later, once you've achieved all of your goals.*

The four fun-loving, butt-kicking, success-inspiring questions are:

1. If time and money were unlimited to me—if I had all the freedom and courage and capital to do ANYTHING I wanted to do—what would I do to leave my mark?
2. If there were no such thing as failure, what life experiences and triumphs would I have?
3. If I won the lottery, would I go to work tomorrow? Would I tell the boss to shove it? And what would my next thought be? After I'd spent a huge chunk of cash on vacations, toys, cars, and homes, what would I commit myself to?
4. What is the craziest, most outrageous rock-star-like fantasy I can imagine myself living?

Is your future coming into focus? You're beginning to walk the walk . . .

To Do:

■ Record the fantasies my four questions inspire.

4. IMPROVE YOUR ASSOCIATIONS

To avoid criticism, do nothing, say nothing, be nothing.
                    —Elbert Hubbard, American writer, editor, and printer

■ SCENARIO

Matt and Jenny have a ton of great friends: Fred's up for parole in a month, Suzy's due for release from rehab, and Bob and Laura haven't kited a check in months.

*Actually, Matt and Jenny's friends are the ones who have great friends: Matt and Jenny. They've been there through thick and thin for their motley collection of inspiring buddies. Here's my point: there's a law of nature that I've seen proved many, many times: **We each resemble a mathematical average of the people we associate most closely with.** Birds of a feather flock together, right?*

■ EXERCISE:

To prove this to yourself, pull out your notebook and do the following:

1. List your five closest friends. Now, estimate the annual income of each. (You have an idea.) Add 'em up. Divide by five.

Whaddya bet your income is right smack-dab in the middle of those of your five closest friends? Why? The old thermostat theory again: We choose friends who are like us. It's time to raise the stakes, to start the motor on your fantasy.

2. Make new friends who are totally kicking ass, living the life you want. Watch your standards and expectations rise to meet theirs.

A good way to do this is to get used to meeting people you're normally uncomfortable spending time with. Take the top salesman at your company to lunch.

Introduce yourself to the speaker at a conference. Finagle your way into a top producer's roundtable. Get to know the owner of the biggest house on your block. You may even find someone willing to mentor you. Buck up and ask to sit in on your mentor's meetings, or ask him to take a look at your work. Exchange ideas. Listen. This is absolutely the most valuable relationship you can have on the road to discovering your vision for yourself.

I'm not saying to ditch your best friend since high school. I know friendships are mighty important and, obviously, you don't pick associations based on financial standing. Just make it a point to make new friends who are growing, learning, and achieving in the direction you want to go.

Now you're talking the talk.

To Do:

- Make new, successful associations.

◼ 5. SURF YOUR LEARNING CURVE

Many are called but few get up.

—Oliver Herford, American writer and illustrator

◼ SCENARIO

John knows that to get ahead at work, he has to be a quick learner, keep up with the times. He wants his personal life to be just as full. He just bought everything he needs to build his own dining room table. Last month he went to a networking seminar. And, recently, he's taken up snowboarding. The problem is he stinks—at all three of these newfound endeavors. He's a sharp guy, but each new skill he attempts is tied to its own set of frustrations. Each has a learning curve that he can't even find, let alone master. So now, John's reluctant to try anything new: he's afraid of failing. He was just beginning to envision his future when self-doubt reared its head, telling him it is too late to learn a new game.

In this day and age, success belongs to those who can adapt and change rapidly, to those who pick up new skills and move forward seamlessly. Whether it's new software, a new sport, or a new business skill, learning quickly is usually the only way we can function; the only way we can adopt the newly acquired skill into our lifestyle.

Why? Well, it seems to me that we are all pressed for time these days. In this time of instant gratification, we frustrate all too easily. If we don't get something right away, chances are we'll drop it like a hot potato. There are just too many things we do well, almost effortlessly, to spend time sucking. (Try snowboarding, for example. Your first day definitely does not impress the chicks.) In order to master something, we have to do it over and over. In order to do it over and over, we have to enjoy it. In order to enjoy it, we must feel like we can do it—and do it well. Which means we have to find at least some success rather quickly.

Sounds hopeless, but I've found a formula for learning that works for me. And it seems to work on **any** new skill I'm trying to pick up in a short time. Whether learning to play the guitar, water ski, speak in public, write poetry, manage money—whatever—I've found that the learning process is remarkably constant.

So, here is my winning formula for mastering your learning curve:

1. **Become a student.** Go to the library, read books on the subject, immerse yourself in its study, attend seminars and workshops, subscribe to magazines on the subject, buy related software or gear, and meet new people who've already mastered the skill. In short, do ANYTHING you can to immerse yourself into the culture of the new skill. You'll be amazed at how quickly you become "one of them." **I can't oversell the importance of this first step. Once you begin to make a habit of this, you'll be amazed at how your facility for learning will climb.**

2. **Find a teacher.** If you are persistent, chances are you'll find someone who's actually excited about taking you under her wing. If you can't find someone in person, read books by respected authorities, follow their careers, and watch them in action. This can absolutely cut years off your progress time.

3. **Jump in.** "Do the thing and you'll have the power," as the saying goes. Commit yourself to looking like a complete goofball the first few times out, and punch your way through it.

4. **Make it a lifestyle.** Once you've jumped in, commit yourself to an hour a day or once a week or every other Thursday—whatever it takes to incorporate your new skill into a lifestyle activity. Once you've made an activity a part of your routine, there's no limit to how far you can take it. Before long, you'll find yourself a master.

That's it. That's the formula. If it works for you, use it. Or add to it, design your own—whatever you have to do to deliver a clear, step-by-step plan of action to your bag of success tricks.

■ **EXERCISE:**

Immortalize your own formula in your notebook, along with the ideas and possibilities it sparks. From my experience, just the simple act of possessing a formula will encourage you to try new things and remove the frustration of not knowing where to begin.

So, let's now relate this to finance:

1. You've become a STUDENT by reading this book. You'll want to find other sources as well.
2. You've found at least one TEACHER (the smartass author of this book, but it's a start).
3. You've JUMPED IN. You've thrown caution to the wind and completed the exercises.
4. You've decided to make financial responsibility a part of your LIFESTYLE.

See? You can do this.

To Do:

■ Record your winning formula in your notebook.
■ Jot down the ideas and possibilities your formula sparks.

■ 6. DEVELOP POSITIVE HABITS

When the well's dry, we know the worth of the water.

—Benjamin Franklin

■ SCENARIO

Jenny is a hard worker. She wakes up at six on weekdays and is always at work by eight. She returns her phone calls promptly, takes lunch at noon, hits the aerobics class by six and is home by eight for dinner. She watches the tube until ten, then hits the hay.

Most of us have a daily routine we follow almost effortlessly. We brush our teeth before bed, we comb our hair from left to right, we say "hello" when picking up the phone, and so on. Here's the point: many of the things we do during the day, we do on "autopilot." We don't have to even think about them anymore, they're just mechanized routine. Still, many of these autopilot habits are quite positive, right?

Take brushing your teeth, for example. It's something you do every day that takes three to five minutes at most. But, still, that's quite an accomplishment: an effortless three-to-five-minute habit offers positive results. However, most of us didn't decide to brush our teeth every night for the rest of our lives the moment our parents mentioned it. They had to teach us, to encourage us, to coerce us, perhaps. But we never forgot and we do it to this day.

"Wealth is largely a result of habit," John Jacob Astor said. So, what if I told you there were financial habits that took three to five minutes a day that would virtually guarantee results? Sure, they'll take a bit of practice at first, but eventually they'll become second nature; eventually they'll become such an ingrained part of your routine that you can go on autopilot, knowing that you're building a secure financial foundation—with virtually no extra effort. Neat, huh?

Now is the time to build those habits that will pave the way to the success we envision.

■ **Exercise:**

Here are fifteen positive financial habits that take no more time than brushing your teeth. Most we'll dissect in later sections, but I want you to become familiar with them. Pick five to begin practicing right away—that's fifteen minutes a day—and write them in your notebook.

Positive Financial Habits (taking three minutes or less):

1. **Write it down.** As you spend money, record every expense and purchase in a notebook.

2. **Pay yourself first.** Save 10% of every dollar you earn as wealth-building capital.

3. **Avoid credit card purchases.** You know this, but especially avoid going in debt for consumables: food, entertainment, transportation, and gifts.

4. **Wait two weeks for major purchases.** If you still want it, get it, but avoid impulse buys.

5. **Review all bills and statements for errors.** You'd be amazed at how often you're overcharged.

6. **Set a time limit on long distance calls.** A lot can be said in just ten minutes.

7. **Read one money-related newspaper article per day.** A year of this, and you've practically earned a finance degree.

8. **Read three pages of a self-improvement book each night.** It's that "slight edge" that makes winners.

9. **Write one thank-you note per day.** Relationships are paramount to success in life.

10. **Plan the following day the evening before.** Having a "game plan" to sleep on maximizes your time and effectiveness.

11. **Maintain only one "master" list or day planner.** Don't waste time looking for phone numbers or misplaced Post-it notes. Get a planner with the works: daily "to do" list pages, an address book, goal-setting pages, heath/fitness/diet tracking pages, check register, and daily journal. Keep your life and finances organized in one book and carry it with you at all times.

12. **Limit your TV viewing time.** It's an alluring, dangerous little box. Hours can slip by if you don't monitor yourself.

13. **Keep a daily journal.** Keep it in the same book as your planner and habitually monitor your effectiveness and life experiences. You will be surprised at how important each day will seem. Who wants to write in their journal, "Didn't do a damn thing today but eat"?

14. **Take action or trash it.** Regarding mail, memos, or notes, forget the "to do" piles. If it's important, do it right now. If not, dump it. Life's too cluttered as it is. You don't want your mind occupied by trivial crap lying around.

15. **Eat an apple a day.** I can't help tossing that in. It really does work wonders for the ol' bod.

Finally, if you are chained by destructive habits, you must find a way to eliminate them and replace them with new, positive habits.

If you do destructive stuff like belittling others, cheating, stealing, pointing undeserved blame, overindulging in food or alcohol, using recreational drugs, overspending heavily, gambling uncontrollably, dwelling on negative thoughts, frowning constantly, saying "I can't" more than twice in your lifetime, watching *any* episode of Gilligan's Island more than, say, three times, still wearing *old* KISS T-shirts under your suit (their new tour stuff is OK), or any other self-defacing practice, please knock it off. Get help if you need to. I'm not kidding. One bad habit can keep you on the "total loser treadmill" if you don't kick it.

To Do:

■ Choose five positive financial habits to practice. Record them in your notebook.

■ 7. Discover What You *Really* Want

Unhappiness is in not knowing what we want and killing ourselves to get it.
—**Don Herold**

■ SCENARIO

Matt and Jenny know they want more financial success: a bigger home, nicer cars, more cash, and more time to spend it. They want to take exotic vacations, own nice things, experience financial security, and all the other exciting, mysterious things they just know more money will bring them. But, so far, this dream life has been avoiding them like the plague. Every step forward is met by two steps back. Every new purchase only whets their appetites: they want something bigger or better almost immediately; fulfillment flirts just out of their reach.

What do Matt and Jenny *really* want? They already have two decent cars, a great pad, appliances, furniture, and most of the other comforts of today's society. Could they have been tricked into believing that "more" and "bigger" are all they *really* want? Matt and Jenny remember how exciting it was to occupy their first home, and driving that first new car off the lot made them feel fantastic. Wouldn't "more" and "bigger" just make them feel that much better?

The answer is NO. In fact, failing to understand this one dynamic is what keeps most people trapped; perpetually stranded on the treadmill of accumulating "things" and "stuff" **while never really getting what they want.**

Here's my point: sometimes **the same level of thinking that got us to where we are is NOT the same level of thinking that will take us where we want to go.**

What Matt and Jenny *really* want is to feel good. What I *really* want is to feel good. What you *really* want is to feel good. Point taken?

But feeling good in today's society can be rather difficult if we let it. We see a shiny new car on a TV commercial and think, "Man, if I could just be cruising down a deserted highway in *that car*, I'd feel great." Or we see a sharp suit of clothes on a model in a magazine and say to ourselves, "I'd feel like a million bucks if I just looked like that." Or we eye a magnificent home in a premium neighborhood and just know that all would be right with the world if we woke up in that home every day.

We've got to be really careful about what or whom we rely on to make us feel good. Do we really have to buy their advertised products to get the feelings we want? Wouldn't **your** present lifestyle make someone less fortunate feel like a complete winner?

What if I told you that right here, right now, you could do an exercise that would release your gums from the marketer's emotional baby bottle? What if I also mentioned that this exercise wouldn't remove your motivation for more and better—it would actually amplify your ability to **achieve greater success** as your perspective alters a bit? Two strong questions, two big claims, but from my experience this section can do all that and more. Are you willing to give it a try?

In the next few paragraphs, I'm going to introduce a concept that might be unfamiliar to you. It might even seem less than specific at times. But just go with me here. I firmly believe that this lesson has impacted me, personally and financially, more than any other I've learned.

Years ago, when I was just starting out, I summed up my drive in one sentence: "I'm money motivated." Perhaps that rings a bell with you as well. Anyway, this idea of being "money motivated" really worked—for a while. Well, **a higher level of success requires a higher level of thought.** It's true. Equally true is the fact that being **only** money motivated is the mark of simple, adequate achievers. It's also a myth. **Nobody is motivated by money.**

I'd better elaborate. Nobody is motivated by numbers and green paper. Not one single person in the world will go to work for numbers and green paper. They won't even get off the couch for it.

We are, however, all motivated by what we *think* these numbers and green paper will give us. **We are motivated by how we think money will make us *feel*.** A fat bank account can make us *feel* **successful, powerful, secure, smart, or sexy** (weird, I know, but think about it). An expensive vacation can give us *feelings* of **adventure, freedom, fun, or independence.** A fine suit of clothes may offer **confidence, beauty, or self-respect.** In this society, we've attached all sorts of compelling *feelings* to the subject of money. We've also attached certain emotions to the lack of money in our lives: **embarrassment, failure, self-pity,** and other schlemiel-like feelings.

Alternatively, some people actually believe they get good feelings by **not** having money. Don't you know people who feel proud about being broke, about not "selling-out" to the money culture? They may say, "I'll be more spiritually connected if I suffer financially," or "I'll be honest and true to my-self if I avoid financial responsibility," or "I'll keep my integrity if I avoid the allure of money," blah, blah blah. That's all crap. That kind of "secondary gain," or what I call the "swap" theory, holds absolutely no water. If you're spiritually connected, you're connected. If you're honest, you're honest. Money will not make or take any of these values from you. You are the only one who can make or take these values from you. This sort of rationalization is simply a lame excuse, a justification for not living up to your guilt-buried potential.

I've thrown in another term on you: *values*. Stepping out of the touchy-feely stuff and into more concrete ground, we're now going to take this new understanding into the realm of the practical.

Feelings are what we want, but we describe and express them through our choice of personal *values*—which encompasses a great deal more. One value can instigate many feelings and actions. For example, don't you know some-one who exercises habitually? Wouldn't it make sense to guess that they value **health** or **challenge** highly? Isn't the workaholic motivated by **power, self-importance,** or by **being needed?** Isn't the social butterfly seeking **acceptance, fun,** or **personal connection?** Isn't the bookworm trying to fulfill the values of **learning, growing,** or **fulfillment?** And isn't the wanderer after **independence** or **adventure?**

I think you get my point: **Our values determine our behavior be-cause we all tend to gravitate to those activities that fulfill those *feelings* we *value* the highest.**

This distinction has all sorts of implications: in sales, we can find our cus-tomer's "hot button." We can understand what draws people together. We can now see why we stick with our favorite activities. And, more important, we can begin to strengthen and redefine our values in order to change our be-havior almost instantly. Once you broaden your thinking, the things you want will become available to you.

If you want to step up your exercise regimen, you'll need to increase your value of **health** or **fitness.** If you want to improve your time-management skills, try increasing your value of **effectiveness** or **being in control.** If you want more money, ascribe **financial responsibility, freedom, power, security,** or **challenge** a higher value.

■ **EXERCISE:**

*In your notebook, write down the **things** you want most right now. Then, re-define those things in terms of values.*

I've found that focusing on my highest values keeps me entrenched in the study and activity of the accomplishment I'm pursuing. And here's the best part: **Instead of feeling good only once you've achieved a goal, you get to feel good by fulfilling your highest values each and every day.** Instead of feeling good only after you've lost that last ten pounds, you get to enjoy **any** activity that fulfills your value of **health.** Instead of rejoicing only after you've made your first million, you get to enjoy the process of any activity that fulfills your value of **security.**

Instead of punishing ourselves daily, sacrificing for an "outcome," we learn to enjoy the "process," which ultimately makes us more successful. We continue only those activities we enjoy—those that make us feel good. Any activity we continue, we tend to master, which ultimately gives us the desired outcome, **while being fulfilled in the process.** Is that friggin' fantastic, or what?

■ **EXERCISE:**

So, let's get to the meat of it: How do we discover our values and make positive changes?

Three steps:

1. **Ask questions.** Learn from someone who's getting the desired result. Chances are, they may not even be aware of what actually makes them tick, so when they explain how they run four miles a day, or make x number of sales calls each week, or vacation six times a year, be prepared to dig a little deeper to uncover their driving values by asking the question: *How do you get yourself to do that?* Once you ask the question, you'll have to pull out their highest values from their reply. They may say something like, "Well, **health** is really important," or "**winning** requires **discipline**," or "I just feel so at **peace** when I'm on the water." These "hidden" values are the real powerful, motivating force behind their achievements. Get the idea?

2. **Refine your own personal values system.** Think about those values that ring *particularly* true for you *right now—those values you feel are essential for a meaningful life.* Begin with the values you discovered among your code of fifteen. Then turn to the list below. Do you

value **acceptance, support, safety, love?** What about **achieve-ment, adventure, freedom, family, or health?** As you consider each value, ask yourself:
"Is _____ essential for a meaningful life?"

Here are some examples to get you started:

__Freedom	__Love	__Excitement
__Security	__Health	__Passion
__Honesty	__Integrity	__Making a difference
__Intelligence	__Being the best	__Fun
__Adventure	__Happiness	__Courage
__Learning	__Growing	__Creativity
__Resourcefulness	__Power	__Family connection
__Respect	__Support	__Confidence
__Beauty	__Humor	__Independence
__Challenge	__Fulfillment	__Self-expression
__Communication	__Wonder	__Acceptance
__Acknowledgment	__Curiosity	__Family
__Spiritual connection	__Peace	__Relationships
__Financial responsibility	__Emotional connection	

Others:

Please notice that **money** is not on the list because it's not a value; it's not a feeling. We want to uncover those values you've attached to money. So don't write down "more money." Take some time to define what it is you **really** want from money—**security, opportunity, freedom,** etc.

3. **Take ownership of your values.** List your ten highest values in order of priority, memorize them, and carry them with you. Now, knowing what's been guiding you, take this moment to OWN your values, to put yourself in charge again. Perhaps you'll want to shuffle them around. Should **health** be higher on the list? Is **freedom** really that important? Or is **security** really more desirable to me now? Does it make sense to value **acceptance** so highly? Or should **self-expression** be paramount instead? You'll be amazed at how simple awareness can pull you toward your desired outcome.

As an example, let me list my top ten highest values. I carry this list every-where, constantly looking for ways to fulfill those values that have significance, those values that make life worthwhile. Every year or so, I update them as my life's priorities shift.

Tod Barnhart's Top Ten Values for 1998

1. Health
2. Relationships/Family
3. Security
4. Balance
5. Communication
6. Doing (active learning)
7. Effectiveness
8. Fun/Adventure
9. Patience
10. Courage

To Do:

- Translate wants into values.
- Ask questions.
- Record your values.
- Prioritize your values.

■ 8. SET DREAM GOALS

There are two things to aim at in life: first, to get what you want; and, after that, to enjoy it. Only the wisest of mankind achieve the second.

—Lloyd Logan Pearsall Smith, essayist

■ SCENARIO

Matt and Jenny agree that their values govern their activities, their habits, and their life. They've determined that, for them, **health, security, relationships, family,** *and* **freedom** *are paramount. But that's where their certainty halts. They are confused, at best, about how to fulfill those values. And the longer they wallow in uncertainty, the more they begin to doubt the whole goofy idea of values in the first place. Pretty soon, they feel, they'll be back into the same old rut if they don't take action and get results NOW.*

Values are the stepping-stones to creating fulfilling, achievable goals. When we make plans and set goals in accordance with our highest values, we can't help but move closer to realizing our dreams. It's called being *congruent*: pursuing the visions that appeal to us naturally and comfortably. Using this value-based approach, you not only identify your true aspirations but also eliminate those that don't serve any purpose.

So let's have some real fun.

■ EXERCISE:

*In accordance with your highest values, define the "things" you'd like to DO, HAVE, SEE, and EXPERIENCE. In your notebook, answer each of the following four questions for **each** of the ten highest values you recorded in the last exercise.*

Wish List

1. "Things" I (and my spouse and/or family) would like to DO:

2. "Things" I (and my spouse and/or family) would like to HAVE:

3. "Things" I (and my spouse and/or family) would like to SEE:

4. "Things" I (and my spouse and/or family) would like to EXPERI-
ENCE:

If you're having trouble, let me offer a couple of examples from my notebook:

Under My Highest Value of HEALTH, Here Is My Wish List:

DO: run the New York Marathon; exercise three times a week; take a
karate class; learn to kayak; eat an apple a day; focus on maintaining a low-fat
diet; and avoid alchohol.

HAVE: a treadmill for indoors; a boxer's heavy bag; a pair of mountain
bikes; a lifetime health club membership; a thirty-two-inch waist forever; a
home gym; and a large fitness/nutrition library.

SEE: attend the Olympics; visit the mountains yearly (maybe skiing or
hiking); see Michael Jordan play live; go to the Super Bowl or the World Series; and attend a triathlon event.

EXPERIENCE: the reward of my clothes fitting loosely; the thrill of
kayaking the Snake River; the speed of a NASCAR race; the beauty of a gym-
nastics meet; and the triumph of achieving my own goals.

Remember, vague goals are useless. Being **specific** leads you to *exactly*
what you want.

Do you see how much more compelling it is to set a financial goal of, say,
buying a treadmill or *attending the Olympics* rather than just wanting "more
money and stuff"? Can you see how you can easily turn away things or activities that take valuable time and resources and would never serve your goals
anyway? Can you see how this offers maximum, fulfilling, financial success?

Here's a more explicitly money-related example:

Under My Highest Value of SECURITY, Here Is My Wish List:

DO: consistently contribute to an Individual Retirement Account (IRA); operate a secure business or vocation; and earn steady pension, medical, and retirement benefits.

HAVE: a warm, comfortable home; three months living expenses in savings; an adequate retirement plan; sound life insurance; an investment holdings nest egg; and a detailed will in effect.

SEE: watch my net worth growing daily; observe a secure, proud expression on my own face; travel the world in first-class accommodations; and witness my children's excitement as they attend the finest universities.

EXPERIENCE: the satisfaction of financial independence; the relief of having complete control over my own time; the power of financial influence; and the glory of prolonging the agony of a boot-licking salesman (in a healthy way, of course).

Questions are amazing tools, aren't they? They help us dream up and create any result we want in life. You can turn a vague idea into a vision of the future and plot a course for its completion by simply answering a few simple questions.

To Do:

■ Record your dream goals for each of your highest values.

■ 9. DEFINE A POWERFUL "WHY"

It's not so much how busy you are, but WHY you are busy. The bee is praised. The mosquito is swatted.

—**Marie O'Connor**

■ SCENARIO

Matt and Jenny had absolutely no idea that monetary success would require such an in-depth consideration of their values, their beliefs, and their dreams. They were prepared to hear, "Memorize this, take this test, fill out this form, wear your best suit and smile, and you'll get the gig." They didn't know it would be so personal. Still, Matt and Jenny are game for financial change. They're willing to try anything that makes sense (unless it hurts or gives them a hickey), and give it an honest effort.

Many times we tend to become lazy, relying on the same old skills that have worked in the past. But, as we've discussed, **the level of thinking that brought us to where we are is not the level of thinking that will take us to where we want to go.** This section is designed to help you harness the *fuel* to achieve your ideal financial vision; the *fuel* to keep you on course on the way to your destiny; the *fuel* to plow through the uncomfortable elements that stand between you and your dreams. What's this *fuel* I'm talking about?

I'm glad you asked. The most powerful internal *fuel* you can possess is a "WHY"—Why are you committed? Why is financial success important? Why is it crucial that you try? Why are you here? Why you?

In my experience, I've found one thing to be absolutely true: **The "WHY" comes first, the "HOW" comes later.** If you can find a strong enough "WHY," you'll find a way to make it happen. And once you learn to uncover your own personal "WHY," you'll find you can't stop yourself from taking positive action: it's too important.

At the root, the most important questions you can answer right now have to do with your own personal **purpose** for existing and succeeding, such as: WHY am I here? **What am I meant to DO, BE, HAVE, ACHIEVE, and GIVE?**

The answers aren't easy to rattle off, I agree. But once your "WHY" is identified, you'll find yourself stronger and more self-certain than ever before. You'll find yourself walking in the world with an air of confidence and possibility. That's the kind of power that comes from having a feet-to-the-center-of-the-earth **clarity of purpose.**

Q: So, what's a **purpose** statement?
A: A purpose is a bold declaration of who you are at the deepest level.

Your **purpose** is your summary of WHY you deserve to live your life in a certain way; an *intentional* declaration of the type of person you are and WHY you want your place in history to be extraordinary. And it always encompasses your highest *values.* (Starting to see a pattern here?)

Most people who spend their lives floating aimlessly **end up following somebody else's plan, taking on somebody else's purpose or none at all, and relying on somebody else's rules for feeling worthy.** As Ralph Waldo Emerson, the nineteenth-century lecturer, essayist, and poet, said, "Luck is another name for tenacity of **purpose.**" The winners of this world don't rely on luck or other people to tell them which mold they should occupy; they rely on themselves for mustering self-confidence. And when things get tough, they get strength from their carefully designed idea of **purpose.** It is their bedrock.

■ EXERCISE:

So this little section is designed to guide you through the process of defining your **purpose,** *the force motivating you to make your mark and bring in the wealth you deserve. From now on, you're not just an actor in your screenplay—you are the producer, the director, and the writer. This is your show. After all, who's more qualified to create your script than you?*

First, let me share my purpose statement with you as an example. I have this written in my planner, repeat it often, and have long since committed it to memory. Can you pick out my highest values?

Purpose Statement, Tod Barnhart:

My "WHY," my purpose in life, is to BE loving, compassionate, courageous, and fun—to move people and have tremendous impact in others' lives—to enjoy myself and graciously accept total abundance in every area of my life. In short, *to live boldly in the zone!*

Yours can be shorter or longer; it doesn't matter, as long as all the ingredients are there. I know people who've simply written *"To be happy!"* or *"To have fun!"* Whatever you decide, remember that this is **your** purpose statement, and it is not to be formed around the expectations of other people. If you have trouble, just ask yourself: **"When all is said and done, how do I wish I'd have lived? How do I want to be remembered?"**

Now you're going to do it. Ready? Here are some guidelines that might help.

1. Begin with, **"My 'WHY,' my purpose in life, is to BE . . ."**
2. It should **encompass your highest values**.
3. Be **specific** only in terms of things you can *be*.
4. Be **general** enough that you can experience it, on some level, just about every day (i.e., nothing like: "To make a million dollars," or "Be the commander of the free world." You need a purpose that's **within your control**, not one measured by external rewards).
5. Think about how you want to interact with and benefit **other people**.

So get busy. Write your statement of purpose in your notebook.

Your statement doesn't have to be grammatically correct, or even sensible to others, for that matter, but it does have to come from your heart. It must be something that stirs you to act, not just an academic exercise. And please don't fall into the trap of thinking that you'll find time to design your life's purpose later. **After all, how much time have you found to devote to this area in the last, say, twenty years of your life?** Let me nag you on this one. I really want you to follow through. This exercise has had such a tremendous impact on my life that I know it will be valuable to you as well.

Now that you're done, answer these questions in your notebook:

1. What realization has my purpose statement prompted?
2. Has my purpose statement shifted my goals? (Refer to your wish list in section 8.)
3. How does it feel to be guided by my own **purpose**, rather than ruled by the plans of others?

To Do:

■ Formulate a purpose statement.
■ Answer the follow-up questions in your notebook.

▪ 10. GET A CLUE

The secret of business is to know something that nobody else knows.

—Aristotle Onassis

▪ SCENARIO

Matt and Jenny are hooked by now. They've done the exercises, implemented every strategy they've learned so far. They've even used their newfound tools to assist them in other areas of their life. Now they want more: more money, more fun, more adventure, more experience, and more time. What they need is more knowledge to keep them always mentally active, always striving, always honing their life visions.

We live in an amazing time. More information is available to the public than ever before. We can surf the Net, go to the dozen libraries in our town, watch educational programs, and participate in seminars, lectures, and continuing education. We have more opportunities for learning, growing, and experiencing life than any other people in history.

Never before in the history of the world have so many people had the chance to benefit from O.P.E.—*Other People's Experience.* We can actually cut decades from our learning time by simply finding mentors and absorbing their time-earned lessons and world experience.

So, below I offer a suggested reading list of the books I've found to have the most impact. Not all are in the area of finance, as you'll notice. Being rich in life is the result of being well-rounded and well-read, tapping into the tree of knowledge. I hope you'll pick up a few and keep on the path to expanding your vision.

SUGGESTED READING LIST

You Are the Message	Roger Ailes
The Platinum Rule	Anthony J. Alessandra
As a Man Thinketh	James Allen
Illusions: The Adventures of a Reluctant Messiah	Richard Bach
Jonathan Livingston Seagull	Richard Bach
Zen and the Art of Making a Living	Laurence G. Boldt
Raving Fans	Ken Blanchard and Sheldon Bowles
Live Your Dreams	Les Brown
The Artist's Way	Julia Cameron
Hero's Journey	Joseph Campbell
The Wealthy Barber	David Chilton
Ageless Body, Timeless Mind	Deepak Chopra
Illuminations	Stephen C. Paul and Gary Max Collins
The 7 Habits of Highly Effective People	Stephen R. Covey
The Story of Philosophy	Will Durant
Self-Reliance	Ralph Waldo Emerson
3 Steps to a Strong Family	Richard and Linda Eyre
The Instant Millionaire	Mark Fisher
Man's Search for Meaning	Viktor E. Frankl
The Poetry of Robert Frost	Robert Frost
Uh-Oh	Robert Fulghum
The E-Myth	Michael Gerber
The Prophet	Kahlil Gibran
Toxic People	Lillian Glass, Ph.D.
Four Screenplays with Essays	William Goldman
Men Are from Mars, Women Are from Venus	John Gray, Ph.D.
Chicken Soup for the Soul (and series)	Jack Canfield and Mark Victor Hanson
A Brief History of Time	Stephen W. Hawking
Think and Grow Rich	Napoleon Hill
Dianetics	L. Ron Hubbard
The Greatest Miracle in the World	Og Mandino
The Making of a Champion	Paul J. Meyer
Way of the Peaceful Warrior	Dan Millman

Get Fit!	Larry North
Beating the Dow	Michael O'Higgins
Unlimited Wealth	Paul Zane Pilzer
How to Be a Great	
Communicator	Nido R. Qubein
Atlas Shrugged	Ayn Rand
The Celestine Prophecy	James Redfield
The Winner Within	Pat Riley
How to Work a Room	Susan Roane
Awaken the Giant Within	Anthony Robbins
Unlimited Power	Anthony Robbins
Seasons of Life	James E. Rohn
Cosmos	Carl Sagan
Do What You Love, the	
Money Will Follow	Marsha Sinetar
Walden	Henry David Thoreau
The Psychology of Achievement	Brian Tracy
The Writer's Journey	Christopher Vogler
Cat's Cradle	Kurt Vonnegut

Additionally, periodicals such as *BusinessWeek, Forbes, Fortune, Time, Money, Newsweek, Success,* and *Entrepreneur* can keep you on the cutting edge of the world of personal finance.

And don't forget: in many cases, the cost of books, magazines, tape courses, workshops, and seminars is deductible if these items relate to your business or career or your personal taxes.

Now you have begun to rewrite your script. You are ready to master the skills you will need to carry out your vision.

To Do:

- Begin building a winning library.

Reality Bites:
Organization and Record Keeping

After refusing to participate in our "shallow economic system," Jenny's tummy begins to growl.

■

If one advances confidently in the direction of his dreams and endeavors to live the life he imagined, he will meet with a success unexpected in common hours.

—Henry David Thoreau

■ 1. GET YOUR LIFE TOGETHER

Dost thou love life? Then do not squander time, for that is the stuff life is made of.
—**Benjamin Franklin**

■ SCENARIO

Matt and Jenny believe they are effective people. Matt recalls most of the mental notes he makes to himself and occasionally jots reminders on Post-it notes. He has a calendar for remembering his family's birthdays and another on his office wall for appointments. Jenny keeps three address books, even though they're a hassle to maintain: one in the kitchen, one on a Rolodex at work, and one on computer. Half their day is spent searching for something one of them "just had in their hand." What neither realizes is that they aren't nearly as effective as they could be; there are skills and habits that would all but eliminate the time they spend looking for notes, addresses, and reminders, freeing them up for the important things.

Most of us don't give a thought to the busywork that fills our day. If we need to call someone, we dig around in our pocketbooks or suit pockets for that cocktail napkin with the number on it. If we need our spouse's Social Security number, we play phone-tag all day. Many times we spend hours searching through papers to find that important idea we jotted down last week. And, worse, we forget birthdays and addresses, and even miss appointments because we're staring at the wrong calendar.

It may not seem like a financial issue, but time management is one of the most crucial skills we can master in today's world. We all have the same amount of time in the day; it's how we use it that makes us effective and wealthy—or not. I'm continually amazed at how many people can't seem to find time for the things they love in life simply because they're wasting hours in a tailspin.

Let me share a personal story. About three years ago, I decided to get in shape. I stuck *Health* on the top of my values list, joined a local gym, bought some new clothes and running shoes, and read several books on diet and health. Within days, however, I found myself swamped with work and missing my workouts. My shoes weren't even broken in yet and I'd already become discouraged by my lack of time and willpower.

One day a friend stopped by to go running (I thought a partner'd get my butt in gear), and I quickly balked, claiming I was too busy. (I was organizing my paper clips or something.) As it so happened, President Clinton was on TV in one of those now famous running clips, jogging down Pennsylvania Avenue. So, my friend says, "Look, the president, a guy with a pretty important job, makes time to jog. Are you telling me you're busier than the president?"

"Yes!" I barked weakly. "I'm . . . I'm . . ." I then realized how ridiculous I sounded. So I picked up my bag and hit the gym. It's been three years now, three of the busiest of my life, and I've kept up my committment to work out at least three times a week, missing hardly ever.

Many times we really do have enough time for the things that are important to us, but we get so focused on the pile of crap that's in front of us we can't see around it. Which is very dangerous, because usually we actually *feel* like we're busy; we *feel* like we're moving forward when we're really just wasting time on trivial activities.

Unfortunately, most of us lack the skills to even *see* where we're spinning our wheels. Luckily, my company at the time of my initiation into health offered a time-management course. Anyone can find a class like this. Anyway, their big thing was: **Write things down ONE time only.** If you make a "to do" list, keep it in your planner; no need to rewrite it every day. If you record someone's phone number, do it in that same place **every time.** Same with ideas, conversation notes, calendar events, and written goals, for easy reference.

Immediately, I got a planner and began pulling my life and my time together. I began by combining all of my calendars into one "master" calendar. Then I completed the pages provided for my goals, values, and priorities. I made space for a daily journal, a health/fitness tracking sheet, a little area for recording daily expenses, and a check register. An address book was inside, as were pages for important information, such as: birthdays, airline and frequent flyer numbers, my wife's Social Security number (which you need a lot more than you'd think if you're married), and her shoe and dress sizes (big payoff if you've got that info). Eventually, I kept my speeches in that "book"—and notes to refer to while on television. I'd walk to the podium, open that book, and—BAM! I'd be ready to rock 'n' roll. If I needed a statistic, flip the page.

A joke, flip another. Want to hear my values and goals as an example? Flip another. A poem I'd feel the urge to recite, there it was. You want to set a meeting? BAM! "Let me check my calendar."

This all combined nicely into one "book" with room for credit cards and keys, and I began carrying it with me everywhere—like a success wallet/organizer/purse sort of thing. Eventually, people started asking about my little planner, and I was amazed at how many had never considered the concept. Even more amazing was that I found myself handling at least ten times more daily activities than I used to. I was juggling TV and radio gigs, my company, and a hectic travel, writing, and speaking schedule. And I was vacationing more and having more time for fun than ever before. It blew me away to think about it. My life altered dramatically once I began to value my time as a precious resource. I can show you years' worth of health/fitness records—the exercises, running times and distance, the food I ate that day; my financial records; gifts bought and received; goals achieved; and a record of how I was feeling, handling challenges, and experiencing life each day.

It's almost sick, I agree. BUT IT WORKS!

So, the moral of the story is this: **However you have to do it, you absolutely must get a grip on your time.** Organize, prioritize, plan, and monitor. Get comfortable turning off the phone or letting it ring if you need space or time. Get in the habit of being a freak about managing **your time** and important information.

One final hint: the second you buy your planner, write your contact information on the front page with a bold statement: REWARD IF FOUND. If you should lose it, you don't want the finder to think twice about doing the right thing. I've only misplaced mine once—at a restaurant—and it was returned, thank God, even though I'd already flown to another city.

To Do:

- Buy a planner.
- Consolidate your lists, notes, and calendars.

◼ 2. ORGANIZE YOUR FINANCIAL DOCUMENTS

In life, as in chess, forethought wins.
—Charles Buxton, British member of Parliament and leader of church reform

◼ SCENARIO

Matt and Jenny both want to get their finances back to manageable. They'd like to have a firm handle on their taxes, their income and assets, and their bills. They both know that they'd feel much better about their situation, even optimistic about the future, if they could just pull their financial loose ends together. As it stands, they're intimidated by the size of the task before them. They're afraid to expose the mistakes they've made or to unpleasantly reveal their "real" financial position. And, anyway, they don't know where to begin. So, day by day, they avoid facing the financial mirror, dreading the day their ducking and dodging will catch up with them.

The worst thing we can do regarding money is to bury our heads in the sand, hoping things will "just work out." Things may usually work out *all right*, but this is not a book about finding mediocrity.

One thing that I believe is important regarding finance and money has to do with how highly our society values OWNERSHIP. Possession is nine-tenths of the law, we've heard. And we all understand the Golden Rule: "He who has the gold makes the rules." But what we often fail to recognize is that OWNERSHIP (wealth) implies a certain level of RESPONSIBILITY. This understanding of ownership, one that our political and economic systems were founded upon, seems relatively foreign to people who haven't achieved a great deal of success yet. So, I'd like you to become familiar with the simple equation: OWNERSHIP = RESPONSIBILITY.

How many people want the boss's income but not the boss's job? Who'd love to own a home but not worry about its upkeep? How many people want the rewards without the effort? It's an alluring prospect, this idea of something for nothing. But it doesn't work. The wealthier the person, the more responsibility they've accepted in exchange. The business owner has employees and payroll to worry about; the buck stops with her. The investor has concerns regarding the proper and most effective use of his capital. And the CEO answers to stockholders. The higher up the ladder you go, the more responsibility you're expected to shoulder.

Is that fair? I don't know, but it seems to me that OWNERSHIP = RESPONSIBILITY is an inescapable law of wealth. It's like you're a parent in some way, a parent to wealth. If you don't watch it, it runs off. If you don't feed it, it dies. If you don't nurture it, it becomes uncontrollable.

■ EXERCISE:

So the first and simplest way to begin accepting responsibility is to simply ORGA-NIZE YOUR FINANCIAL DOCUMENTS in an accessible place. It's a small thing we can all do immediately that yields powerful results; it forces us to accept where we are now—good or bad—while encouraging us to grab the reigns firmly, going forward. Here's a sample organizing system:

1. **Set up a place** for your filing system. Use manila file folders and a file cabinet for storage.

2. **Label each folder** according to category:

   Bank and brokerage account statements   *Creditors*
   Important papers   *Insurance*
   Tax returns (maintain at least seven years) *Medical bills*
   Investment holdings   *IRAs*
   Monthly expenses (rent, telephone, utilities, *Mortgage info*
       and so forth)
   Expenses/receipts (write dates, locations, and
       business purposes on all receipts)

3. **Mark in your calendar** the payment due dates for all your bills. Late payments harm your credit rating. A calendar avoids the crisis-response of "shut-off" notices and the expense of "late payment fees."

4. **Request "coupons"** from all your creditors that offer them. You probably received a coupon booklet when you took out a car loan or a mortgage. It's a booklet of tear-out pages that has all the pertinent information regarding your loan: lender's address, account number, pay-

ment amount and due date, and so on. Mailing this "coupon" with your payment assures you the fastest processing, which avoids late fees and bad credit notations. Coupons are available for student loans, lines of credit, mortgages, auto and boat loans, even credit cards, in some cases. They want to make it easy for you to send them your money. Use their services.

5. Keep an accurate check register. Nothing aggravates a banker more than an annoying call regarding a charge you want to dispute. Usually, the customer failed to keep accurate records or just forgot where they wrote checks and spent money. I know there are exceptions, but banks have extremely sophisticated accounting software and systems. They are not in the business of ripping you off clearing a nonexistent check for fifty bucks to The Gap. If you write the check, write it in your check register immediately, AT THE POINT OF PURCHASE, as you write the check. Oh, and this banker you've been annoying with time-wasting queries? Chances are she'll be across the desk when you're applying for a car or home loan. So be respectful. They're sticklers for organization; if you want their favor, you should be, too.

To Do:

- Create a filing system.
- Mark payments due in your calendar.
- Request payment coupons.
- Keep your checkbook up-to-date.

In the following sections, we'll raise the bar a bit by getting really specific, even preparing your **personal financial statement,** which you'll need when dealing with banks and lenders. But the first step to getting a firm grip on your financial life is to organize your records. Don't just do it once; make organization a part of your routine. Once you have a system in place, it takes only a few minutes a month to keep organized and a few seconds to find the information when you need it. Plus, this organization makes a firm statement about how you're now willing to accept OWNERSHIP going forward, how you're ready for more RESPONSIBILITY and more financial success.

■ 3. LIST YOUR DEBTS AND CREDITORS

Let us all be happy, and live within our means, even if we have to borrow the money to do it with.

—Bishop William Warburton

■ SCENARIO

Matt and Jenny have debts like everybody else. They usually pay off their credit card bills in full each month, but the whole idea of owing—auto, mortgage, student loans, department store cards—has become convention. They'd like to be debt-free, but, truthfully, they just don't see how it can happen. Everyone they know owes somebody something, and it seems like credit card spending is a way of life in America. "Doesn't everybody have a few debts?" they wonder. "Or owe on their cars and home? Isn't that normal?"

Unfortunately, the answer is yes. Debt is becoming a normal constant in most people's lives, but that doesn't make it right, or healthy. Throughout history, people have willingly given over their economic power to creditors. Well, historically, relatively few people have lived extraordinary lives. Many have chosen to live an average existence, never taking control of their destiny.

Only two percent of the U.S. population has achieved what they would consider financial success. Negligence is a rotten excuse for mediocrity. I believe that we all have the ability to excel far beyond even our wildest dreams, especially living in America.

I've been fortunate enough to have traveled a bit, most memorably to the Far East: China, Hong Kong, Japan, Thailand, and Korea. For nearly a month, I visited these distant lands with excitement, but nothing would prepare me for what I saw: poverty, crowds, police-controlled states. The absence of opportunity. And these are developed nations just like ours with cities and shopping malls and running water.

Most of us have no idea how truly fortunate we are to live in America. Because of our good fortune, I believe we have the responsibility to succeed, to improve our quality of life and that of future generations, to set a benchmark of possibility for the rest of the world. Pollyanna? Whatever. I just believe it's our duty to wisely use what we've been given.

One of the things that actually takes opportunity and freedom from us is debt. It keeps people in dead-end jobs, creates depression and loss of ambition, ruins marriages, and keeps us continually operating in survival mode as we struggle to pay the bills, never embracing the life we might have had.

Consequently, I'd like to encourage you to get out of debt and stay out of debt. It seems like a small thing, but it can literally change your outlook and experience of life when you have to answer to no one financially. Your whole idea of what's possible for you expands as you release yourself from the slavery of debt.

So, here's the first step toward living forever debt-free: LOOK IT IN THE EYE. Face your debts, determine EXACTLY whom and how much you owe, then you can work toward eliminating this crippling burden.

■ EXERCISE:

For starters, in your notebook, LIST YOUR DEBTS AND CREDITORS. Then create a separate file in your new system for each of your obligations, such as:

- *Department store cards*
- *Gas cards*
- *Credit and charge card accounts*
- *Student loans*
- *Auto and boat loans*
- *Personal or home equity loans*
- *Parents (who doesn't owe them at least something?)*
- *And so on . . .*

Then make an information page for each file, including all the relevant stats: terms of the loan, interest rates and charges, total balance due (if you don't pay them off in full each month), and so on. As you make a payment, note that on your information page as well. Write the total balances due from each account in your notebook as well.

Next, add them up. Calculate your total debt . . . C'mon. Look that number straight in the eye and know that you can handle it. It's not that bad. Keep your total debt figure handy so we can use it to prepare your **net worth statement** later. Don't be afraid: *most people overestimate their debt load and* *way, way, way underestimate their assets.* It's a pessimistic little phenomenon, but you'll probably do the same. The good news is that you're going to feel really great in a few pages, so hang in there.

In the meantime, begin to settle your accounts. Call your creditors with balance queries or if you're behind on the payments. Explain that you intend to keep your commitment but perhaps you can only pay a certain amount right now. They'll work with you if you're having a tough time. They may complain at first, but they'd rather have you communicating and paying *something* than avoiding their letters and calls. Then, set up payment plans that you can afford and stick to them.

You'll be amazed at the financial freedom that you experience from just *deciding* to knock those haunting debts down to size.

To Do:

- List your debts and creditors in your notebook.
- Make a file for each.
- Make an info page for each file.
- Record your balance due for each in your notebook.
- Add it up and face the music.
- Develop a payment plan.

■ 4. LIST YOUR ASSETS

When a fellow says, "It ain't the money but the principle o' the thing," it's the money.
—**Abe Martin**

■ SCENARIO

Matt and Jenny have now got a handle on their debts and have set some financial goals. Still, they feel less than certain about their future; they're not even sure the present is all that great. It seems like they're continually saying "no" to themselves regarding things they want to buy or trips they want to take. Every time they sit down to pay the bills, they find themselves short or just barely breaking even. It's frustrating. They've been working for some time and don't feel like they really have anything to show for it.

Many times we tend to focus on what we **don't have** instead of appreciating what we **do have.** It's an easy trap to fall into because our appetite for moving forward is so deep-seated. I've found one simple exercise that helps put things into perspective. Once a year or so, LIST YOUR ASSETS on paper. This is extremely valuable in terms of learning to appreciate how much you really have accumulated. It's also very useful because your assets list will become a part of your **personal financial statement,** which we'll create next, and you'll certainly need it when dealing with banks and other lenders. This list will also become an important part of your homeowner's or renter's insurance file.

■ EXERCISE:

There are several things you'll need to do to put your assets list in order:

1. **Make a list of your *tangible* assets.** List everything you own on a designated page in your notebook. Include all of your assets: liquid assets (savings and investment accounts, mutuals funds, and cash), furniture, stereo equipment, expensive clothes, computers, athletic equipment, lawn equipment, jewelry, works of art—everything. Don't just list items generically; also include **brand names** and serial or **model numbers,** if applicable. And—this is important—also include your estimate of **each item's value.** Photocopy the list.

2. **Take photos of your assets.** Buy a disposable camera if you don't own a good one and take decent pictures of the furniture and appliances inside of your home, as well as the clothes and equipment in your closets or garage in case of theft or fire. Your homeowner's or renter's insurance policy should protect you against loss or damage, but you don't want to be in the awkward position of justifying the extent of your loss without accurate records. It's tough to recall every single possession you own, especially if it's not around when you file your claim. If you have access to a video camera you can tape an audiovisual running narrative, instead of still photos, by verbally stating information about the asset as you record.

3. **Store your photos and list together.** Keep your photos (or videotape) with the copy of your assets list in a fireproof safe or safety deposit box at a bank. You should keep other important papers, such as property deeds, auto titles, marriage certificates, wills, passports, and birth certificates in the same safe place. It's no good if your records burn down with the place.

4. **Make a list of your *intangible* assets.** Finally, make a list of intangible assets you possess, such as: *creativity, enthusiasm, experience, warmth, humor, dedication,* and *honesty.* Then take a minute to write a few sentences recalling times when you've exhibited these qualities and how they benefited you and other people. This won't impress your banker, I agree, but in terms of building wealth, most of the assets you'll need—commitment, vision, and perseverance—have nothing to do with numbers. Buildings aren't erected, companies aren't formed, movies aren't made, nor empires built simply because someone has a pile of cash lying around. These visions come to life because someone **possessed tremendous *intangible* assets that were conta-**

gious enough to rally the *tangible* support. Think about that for a minute; I think you'll agree that these intangible assets form the bulk of our potential and, therefore, the bulk of our wealth.

To Do:

- List your tangible and intangible assets.
- Photograph your valuables.
- Store these photographs and a copy of your assets list in a safe place.

■ 5. PREPARE YOUR PERSONAL FINANCIAL STATEMENT

Property is the fruit of labor; property is desirable; it is a positive good in the world. That some should be rich shows that others can become rich and, hence, is just encouragement to industry and enterprise.

—Abraham Lincoln

■ SCENARIO

Matt and Jenny are beginning to get the hang of this. They've kept up with the exercises, and they're starting to get a feel for where they really stand. But they don't know how to express their position to anybody on the outside—and that's about to become very important.

When dealing with banks and other financial institutions, it is absolutely imperative that you learn to speak their language. There's so much power in being seen as "one of them" when applying for credit or special services. The professionals who work for these institutions are accustomed to simplified financial data sheets called **personal financial statements.** If you walk into their office without one, you've immediately put yourself at a disadvantage. Here's their rationale: "I've seen six deadbeats today asking for loans, all too uninformed to even complete a simple financial statement. Oh, here's my next appointment. They don't have a financial statement so they must be just like all the others."

Is that fair? Probably not, but it's only human nature to make such assumptions. After all, the wealthy or reliable clients that the bank desires all seem to have their financial affairs organized. Anything else implies irresponsibility, which is a definite buzz kill to a banker.

By the way, if you don't think you'll ever need a banker on your team, you may want to rethink that idea. If you plan on owning a home, running a business, buying a new car, or investing and accumulating wealth, you're going to need a team of people from the industry on your side. Here's the good news, though: they sincerely want to help and have the experience and tools (not to mention the money) to help you achieve your dreams. But they have to report to their superiors just like everyone else. So, you need to become familiar with their practices.

Anybody who's anybody in the world of money has had to prepare a personal financial statement at one time or another. At it's simplest, it's just a one-page snapshot of your net worth on any particular day.

Here's the formula:

$$\frac{\text{ASSETS (what you } \textit{own}) \quad - \text{ LIABILITIES (what you } \textit{owe})}{= \text{YOUR \textbf{NET WORTH} (the difference)}}$$

One of the biggest mistakes people make is assuming that having **no statement** is better than having a **"bad" statement**. That's so wrong. First off, just about everyone feels at least a little insecure about revealing themselves in this way. We all think we should be doing "better"; that our financial picture is "bad." But remember, bankers and financial people deal in realities. It's their job to find out exactly where you stand in terms of assets and liabilities. They'll check your credit report and payment history. They'll uncover your income, and their experience will give them a pretty good idea of your expenses. They'll find out EXACTLY where you are, so help them do their job. A thorough financial statement says that you understand what they want, which makes them more eager to help you get what you want.

■ EXERCISE:

So, take your figures from the previous sections: LIABILITIES (debts, creditors) and ASSETS (tangible only—they don't want to hear how cheerful *and* creative *you are), and complete a one-page PERSONAL FINANCIAL STATEMENT. List your LIABILITIES (probably better to leave out the room-and-board you owe Mom) and your ASSETS (be sure to include your **liquid assets**—your savings and investment accounts, mutuals funds, and cash) very thoroughly; more information is better. I'm telling you, they'll find it, so you may as well initiate some standard of trust right off the bat. Show them you're organized. That will tell them the situation is under control. Next, run the numbers to come up with a CURRENT NET WORTH figure. Use the **Personal Financial Statement** form as a template.*

Assets		Liabilities	
LIQUID ASSETS		MORTGAGE LOANS	
Cash accounts	$	Home	$
Bonds	$	Vacation home	$
CDs	$	Investment property	$
Mutual funds	$		
Stocks	$	INSTALLMENT LOANS	
Cash value life	$	First auto	$
Other	$	Second auto	$
Total liquid assets	$	Furniture	$
		Credit cards	$
FIXED ASSETS			
Home	$	OTHER	
Real estate	$		$
Furniture	$		$
Audio/video equip.	$		$
Jewelry	$		$
Art	$		
		Total Liabilities	$
Sporting equip.	$		
Boat	$		
Autos	$		
Motorcycle	$	**Net Worth Calculation**	
Retirement programs	$		
Business value	$	Total Assets	$
Other	$	minus	
	$	Total Liabilities	$
	$		
	$	**Current**	
Total Fixed Assets	$	**Net Worth**	$
Total Assets	$		

To Do:

■ Complete **Exhibit 1** to prepare your **personal financial statement**.

■ 6. CREATE A FINANCIAL GOALS SECTION IN YOUR NOTEBOOK

A goal is a dream with a deadline.

—Steve Smith, Amdahl Corporation

■ SCENARIO

Matt and Jenny are becoming excited by the prospect of a brighter financial future as they take important steps toward the realization of their goals. One of the things they've not done, however, is set a practical time frame for each goal; nor have they gotten specific, in actual dollars, as to what it'll take to achieve their idealized financial life. Consequently, they've just begun to tap into the power of goal setting; it'll take one more step to turn their dreams into reality.

We know that in order to hit the target we must first define it concretely and specifically. Since goal setting is so powerful and we know it works, I am continually amazed at how few people actually take the time to do it. Most people agree on how important goal setting is, but when asked for their own written goals, they haven't bothered to really think them out.

■ EXERCISE:

Please don't fall into that trap. Don't put off this powerful exercise. Instead, take the action now. (You know you need to do it.) Harness that momentum you've already begun building by plotting a serious, achievable course toward higher success. The back of an envelope or a scrap of paper is not the ideal place to formulate your life's financial plan. So, in your notebook, follow the steps below.

1. List *all* your financial goals.
2. Divide your goals into the following categories:

Income
Net worth
Achievement
Possession
Experience

Under each category, list:
a) Your financial **goals** (use specific numbers where possible);
b) The **target date** for achieving them; and
c) A few powerful **reasons** you're committed to these goals. Remember, "Why" comes first, and "How" comes later. Remember your top values when examining your reasons.
3. Now, goal by goal, design your specific *plan of action.* Start with the **target date** you've set for their completion, then work backward, listing the *daily, weekly,* and *monthly* actions you are going to take on the road to its attainment.

Any time you set a new goal, find at least one action you can take right away. This habit builds up that all-important momentum.

Here's an example. Let's say that, under *Possession,* you've listed *owning a gold watch* as one of your major **goals.** Let's also assume that you've given yourself a **target date** a year away. As compelling **reasons** for achieving your goal, you've written: "I want to own a gold watch so that I will feel successful and powerful, so that anyone can see at a handshake that they're not dealing with a kid." Next, you'll want to list specific activities you can do, **right away,** that will lead you toward the goal. For example: 1) *Today,* I'll begin to ask people I respect what kind of watch they wear. 2) *Within the week,* I'll shop around, learn the lingo, and develop an eye for price and quality. 3) *Within the month,* I'll identify the watch I want. 4) *Every week,* I'll put a percentage of the money away, earmarked just for this purchase. 5) *After six months,* check your progress. Are your weekly contributions going to buy you the prize in a year's time?

Simple, right? That's a solid plan for buying a gold watch within your **target date.** Notice that we've thrown in opportunity for refiguring and monitoring. That's important because life doesn't always go according to plan. After four months, if all hasn't gone perfectly, you can reevaluate and take, say, fourteen months to buy the watch if you need the extra time. Still, you've kept to your plan for four months and continue to have a sound plan going forward. Don't make the mistake of losing interest or motivation if you don't stick exactly to your plan. You're human. But if you keep your goals in front of you and maintain a plan, you can't help but arrive at your destination.

4. Make it a habit to **review your major goals daily.** The details you will want to review weekly, at least.

5. **Give your major goals "nicknames"** so you can memorize them easily. For example: "Debt free, whoopee!" or "New home, big as the Astrodome," or "New car'll take me far." Be silly if you have to. Have fun. Enjoy the process of attaining your goals. It's so powerful to be able to crack a smile when you think of your goals. They become compelling and fun rather than onerous. Get the idea?

6. As you **achieve each goal,** write the word ACHIEVED and the DATE achieved in big bold letters diagonally across the entry. It's incredible how much momentum even the smallest success can carry.

To Do:

- Set specific, concrete financial goals.
- Design a plan of action, starting **TODAY.**

◼ 7. CREATE SEPARATE ACCOUNTS FOR EACH GOAL

Knowing what your goal is and desiring to reach it doesn't necessarily bring you closer to it. Doing something does.

—George Eld

◼ SCENARIO

Matt and Jenny are willing to put in the effort to make their money dreams come true. They try to set aside savings for the things they want in life, but, at the end of the month, their resources always seem to be committed to other priorities. They try to enjoy at least some of their money, but they always seem to end up dipping into their fun money to handle other expenses.

◼ EXERCISE:

The best way I know to stay on course is to set up a **separate investment account** *for each dream or goal. Do this for each of the major gaols you recorded in the last section. Subtitle each account according to its purpose: home down payment, vacation, new sports car, children's education, and so on (e.g.: Matt and Jenny Sherman, property account). This way, you won't be tempted to commingle funds and lose track of your original intent. Maybe you have to wait a month for that new suit because the money's already been designated for your anniversary vacation, which was at one time important enough to require a separate account.*

Remember, it's so easy to dribble away our economic power for short-term gratification, thereby forgoing our truest long-run desires. Marketers excel at pushing our buttons through sales, promotions, and the like; many times, things we think we need aren't really priorities in saner moments. Creating separate accounts for each goal forces you to recall your highest priorities and dreams. You can actually have *more* of what you want by learning to say "no" to the impulse purchases. And the payments on that new "bargain" sports car won't squeeze the resources for your kid's education or the down payment on a home.

To Do:

- Set up separate accounts for each financial dream.

■ 8. KEEP ALL RECEIPTS

That which we persist in doing becomes easier for us to do; not that the nature of the thing itself has changed, but that our power to do is increased.

—Ralph Waldo Emerson

■ SCENARIO

Matt and Jenny are burning money and they don't even know it. Matt spends personal money on computers and books that he uses exclusively for business. Jenny's job requires special clothes, which she pays for out of her own pocket. And, from time to time, they entertain co-workers and customers at home or at restaurants for business purposes.

We're going to discuss tax deductions in later sections, but this strategy has awesome benefits at every stage. Habitually saving every single receipt is an excellent way to save yourself big bucks at tax time—you can deduct most work-related expenses and, in some cases, even a part of your housing and utilities costs if you maintain an office at home. Keeping your receipts ensures that you don't overlook them at tax time (they're usually larger than you think, over a year's period). Plus, you'll need the proof in case you're audited.

Those benefits are big enough, but there's another: **keeping every receipt forces you to look every dollar you've spent squarely in the eye.** (Posting those expenditures in a planner puts them right in your face, but we'll discuss that later, too. Still, you need receipts to do it right.) It's tough to ignore your goals if your actions remind you daily whether you're on track or not.

Get in the habit of asking for a receipt for everything—not just deductible expenses—because you (and the IRS) want to know that you don't spend every dime on work-related stuff. Find a box or a file that you can use exclusively for receipts and get a new one every year. Once you get into the mind-set of keeping a "paper trail" of your money, you'll be amazed at how many of the things you buy are really "investments" in your job or business.

To Do:

- Keep every receipt for five years—habitually, always and forever. And then some.

9. HABITUALLY INQUIRE ABOUT DISCOUNTS AND SALES

The chief value of money lies in the fact that one lives in a world in which it is overestimated.

—H. L. Mencken

■ SCENARIO

Matt and Jenny enjoy nice clothes, cars, and furniture. They usually shop around for the best deals, if they have time, and try to avoid overpaying if they can help it. They've tried discount warehouses and shopping clubs. Still, they're amazed at how expensive some things can be and wonder if there isn't a way to save even more money, which would help them reach other goals.

Three stories to illustrate:

A few years back I walked into a music store to buy some guitar gear. The salesman loaded me up and offered me a 20% discount, like it was nothing. After talking, I found out that most of their customers were musicians (duh!) who were basically broke. In order to move merchandise, they'd developed an unwritten policy of offering a discount rather that let a customer walk. After that, I never wore a suit into a music store. Now, I putter around and act freaked out by the "high prices" and almost always get a discount, which they're happy to extend; it's normal.

Lately, we remodeled our home, and my wife and I did a large part of the work in our spare time. Over the course of a month, we must have gone into hardware and furnishing stores about fifty times, buying doorknobs, paint, and frilly, decorative crap. So, on about our second trip into these stores, I summoned the sales manager and let him know that we'd be needing a lot of supplies for a while. "And rather than going to another store, which happens to be closer and keep better hours," I said (always find a subtle way to mention their competition), "we'd like to do business with you." I mentioned that I'd heard that some of their larger, corporate customers received discounts and wondered if they could do the same for us. BINGO! We were set up in the computer for a 10% discount on anything, permanently.

My wife and I vacationed in Jamaica for our honeymoon. We'd taken a day trip to Dunn's River Falls and wore only our swimsuits; I'd only stuffed a fifty-dollar bill into my trunks. (How many coconut drinks can you buy in an afternoon?) The falls were a bona fide tourist trap with vendors and artists crawling all over the place, and right off the bat, we came across a magnificent work of art: an eight-foot giraffe sculpture, fashioned by hand from a single trunk of a palm tree. It was absolutely fabulous! Asking price: three hundred U.S. greenbacks. Well, I only had that fifty, and these folks don't take Visa, you know? I knew we wouldn't be coming back because it was a three-hour trip across the island, so I explained to the artist that I loved his work but didn't bring enough money. I was really sorry, but I couldn't afford it. Well, he began his pitch, and long story short, we bought this awesome piece for fifty bucks! Plus we bummed some beef-jerky because we had no money left for food. (Getting an eight-foot giraffe home on the plane, then through customs was another story.)

Moral: **everything's negotiable.** If you want a discount, ASK. Many times, you'll get it.

Most of us think that negotiating is only possible with cars, homes, and salaries. But I've found that you can get almost anything at a discount: hotel rooms, lumber, office supplies (found a slightly nicked desk for a hundred bucks, not four hundred), and just about anything else.

So, if you feel uncomfortable asking for price breaks, two things:

1. **Get over it.** It's *real* money we're talking about, cash that you could use for other things. Drop the "Mr. Big Bucks" attitude. Money humbles us all, know that. So don't be an idiot; leave your ego at home.
2. **They want your money.** The retailer or business you've entered needs your granola to make it. They've got their stuff marked up sky high so they can cash in on the few items that do sell. They want to move the merchandise fast. So 20% off is fine by them. Cash flow, get it?

To Do:

■ Ask for discounts. Always.

■ 10. CONSIDER MONEY MANAGEMENT SOFTWARE

If you think education is expensive—try ignorance.

—Derek Bok

■ SCENARIO

Matt and Jenny have bitten the bullet and gotten their financial documents in pristine order. Thing is, they haven't seen daylight in weeks. It was a big job and, barring Matt's acquisition of "Rain Man's" number skills, they're afraid they won't be able to sustain such organizational endurance going forward.

I've used a couple of software programs that prompted near-religious experiences, Microsoft Money and Quicken, and I'm faithfully seeking others.

Here's my suggestion: find money and/or financial-planning software that you're comfortable with, and use it. If you don't have access to a computer, then, by all means, get access. Or simply buy a horse and buggy and throw in the towel, 'cause you're way outta your times, baby.

These programs save valuable time and . . . blah, blah, blah. If these computers can digitally morph your face into that of a jackass, what do you think they can do with a checkbook? They're awesome.

To Do:

- ■ Computerize your financial record-keeping.
- ■ Digitally morph your own face into that of a jackass, just for fun.

CHAPTER

3

20,000 Leagues Under the Sea:
Controlling Credit Card and Debt Expenses

Matt and Jenny open their eyes and revoke their boycott on financial responsibility, only to find that their creditors had been keeping tally all along.

Out of the lowest depth there is a path to the loftiest height.

—Ralph Waldo Emerson

■ 1. KNOW THE *REAL* COST OF BORROWED MONEY

I'm living so far beyond my income that we may almost be said to be living apart.
—e. e. cummings

■ SCENARIO

Matt and Jenny are now number-crunching fools. They've faced down their total debt figure and understand the monthly interest they're throwing away to lenders and credit card companies. But what's the real cost of their borrowing habit? They know they'll have to repay the principal balance and the interest charges and any other service charges their creditors care to tack on, but is that really all their over-spending is costing them?

One concept from business school that actually made sense to me is defined by the term *opportunity cost*. The concept implies that **every purchasing decision we make comes at the expense of another option.** If you just laid down big dinero for a new car, that money is now tied up; it can't be used for investment capital, the down payment on a home, or higher education. That money won't have doubled in seven years (which is reasonable investment performance), it won't become valuable equity in your home (like a sizable down payment would), and it won't be available to help you seed that business, learn a new skill, or change professions. Considering all this, what did that new car really cost you? What's the *opportunity lost?*

Consider the *opportunity cost* or *lost* before you purchase anything big. Before major buying decisions, write down all the things this new purchase will *cost* you, the things you'll have to forego if you make this decision. Many times, just the consideration of the *opportunity cost* or *lost* concept will help you make sound choices. Once you have this measuring stick and can relate it to actual items (car vs. business, for example), you'll find yourself more in control. After all, a new car is nice, but what would happen if you used that capital (or monthly payment amount) as a conduit to your dreams? Usually our truest priorities carry so much more emotional weight that we wouldn't think of trading them for chrome and steel—or a myriad of credit card charges. But first, you've got to realize the real swap you're making.

To Do:

- Use *opportunity cost* or *lost* as a spending barometer.

■ 2. ERASE YOUR CREDIT CARD DEBT

Man must choose whether to be rich in things or in the freedom to use them.

—Ivan Ilych

■ SCENARIO

Matt and Jenny have a problem. Their credit spending has become near uncontrollable because it's so easy to just whip out their cards without really thinking. It's always for something they need, *of course—at the moment. They've made credit cards a part of their life, and they aren't about to let them go. Do they have to live in credit card debt forever?*

The only way to ever be free from credit card debt is to STOP. NOW. Stop spending future income and learn to live on, and enjoy, your present economic level. Then and only then will you be able to completely ERASE YOUR CREDIT CARD DEBT.

It's so frustrating to watch people on the credit card roller coaster. Just when they're about to get flush, they get another "preapproved" credit card offer in the mail; before you know it, they're back in a nose dive. So, here are some tips for managing your credit card spending and debt (and the horrendous feelings of despair, helplessness, and fury that accompany such financial self-mutilation):

1. **Pay off consumables every month.** If you feel you must use your credit card, make sure you pay off "consumables"—things that perish, such as meals, entertainment, and trips—each month. Remember, only tangibles add to your net worth, so avoid paying finance charges for things that don't add to your assets. Even then, only put off payment if you've considered the *opportunity cost* involved. For example, furni-

ture might be a reasonable charge if you need it, but a round of drinks for your softball buddies is not.

2. **Shop for cheaper credit card interest rates and charges.** If you have good credit, you can qualify for credit cards with rates as low as six or seven percent, or maybe lower. Just make sure there aren't any substantial hidden charges, such as *prepayment charges* (if you pay off your balance promptly), excessive *annual service charges* or undue *statement fees*.

3. **Compare "low fee" cards with those that offer a "low rate."** Credit card companies make their money in basically two ways: *1) Fees*—annual fees, maintenence fees, membership fees, statement fees, prepayment fees, and so on, and *2) Interest rate charges*—by far the largest, most profitable charges in their business. So, shop around. If you maintain large balances (that they can charge you interest on), ask for their program with the lowest *rates*. If you pay off your bill as it comes due (thereby depriving the corporate machine the ability to milk you queasy), you may want to find a program with lower maintenance *fees*. But understand, cards with the lowest *fees* usually carry the highest *rates*—and vice versa. They've gotta make their green somewhere and are determined to get it from you one way or another.

4. **Use a "no-fee" credit card** if you pay off your balance each month. Sometimes, in an attempt to get their paws on your interest-accumulating balance, credit card companies will offer a "no-fee" credit card program. If you can get it, that's ideal. *If* you pay on time. That sort of program usually carries the highest interest rates. And be advised: in my experience, these "no fee" offers are the ones most likely to sell your name to other phone solicitors, who try to sell you products that you'll most likely charge on their card. So if you do accept "no-fee" offers, request they not sell or trade your name to any other marketers.

5. **Double your monthly payments** to get out of debt in half the time. Most people think that if they just pay the stated monthly "minimum payment" then they're doing fine. Surely the credit card company has calculated the best way for you to get out of debt, right? WRONG. The credit card company has calculated the most profitable payment schedule for THEM: a monthly minimum they think you can meet, while incurring the maximum interest charges on your unpaid balance. Paying only the minimum ensures that you'll help finance the bank president's new Lear jet and you will never, never get out of

debt—EVER! Their interest compounds so that you're eventually pay-ing "interest on the interest," which multiplies faster than free-range rabbits. They don't want you out of debt; they want you making the payments and paying their salaries. Get it? Do you really? Then make **double payments**, or more, and get their hooks out of you!

Making **double payments** ensures that at least half of your money is going to pay down the principal, which they can't stand. (BEWARE: they'll raise your credit limit if you do this, thus allowing you to get deeper in debt. Watch and see.)

To Do:

- Take steps to erase credit card debt.

■ 3. USE A DEBIT CARD INSTEAD OF CREDIT

Don't stay in bed . . . unless you make money in bed.

—**George Burns**

■ SCENARIO

Matt and Jenny both know debt stinks. They really would like to eliminate credit cards from their lives altogether, but it's tough. Credit cards are a convenient payment option, sometimes the only option. Jenny travels often, relying on her credit card for hotel, car rental, and air fare expenses. Matt buys gifts and merchandise by mail, on-line, and from TV. As hard as they try to avoid borrowing, they continually find themselves paying hefty Visa bills and the accompanying charges and interest.

Before we get too much farther into this section on credit and debt, let me just say: I don't like credit cards. (Which you must've already sensed, unless you've been asleep.) I've gotten into trouble with them in the past and know how awful it feels to just make that minimum payment, thereby getting royally screwed by the finance charges. Since credit cards are so easy to flash and the charges can pile up so quickly, many people find themselves buried, trapped by overwhelming credit card debt quicker than they can say "hog-tied."

An excellent solution: run, don't walk, to your local bank and open an account that offers a Visa debit card. The charge-like card looks, feels, and works just like a credit card, but it's better: the charge is a nearly instant "debit" from your account, not a loan. Just like writing a check, except faster and more convenient, the charge amount is deducted from your account. You get convenience, all the Visa goodies, and avoid borrowing (and all the crap that goes with it). It's a *good* thing.

To Do:

- ■ Call your bank about getting a debit card.

◼ 4. DEVELOP POSITIVE DISCIPLINES

My problem lies in reconciling my gross habits with my net income.

—Errol Flynn

◼ SCENARIO

Matt and Jenny already possess decent money-management habits. They pay their bills on time, try to stick to a budget, and are constantly learning new skills and developing more effective routines. But they do want to enjoy their life and money and, from time to time, find themselves allured by impulse buys in weak moments. But, that's no big deal, they think. These "weak moment" purchases aren't affecting them that much, right?

We all buy frivolous stuff, at times. Usually, it really is no big deal and doesn't substantially affect our financial standing in the least. Sometimes, however, impulse spending **is** a problem, and we just don't realize it. That's the nature of *dribble spending*: the money's gone before we can really assess what's happened. A problem arises when we **habitually** make "unconscious" buying decisions: a certain magazine purchased at the checkout counter (on *every* trip to the store); the "on-sale" clothing items that we can't seem to avoid; the piecemeal monthly commitments we make, like additional cable TV services, that seem insignificant in the moment; or the boredom-inspired knickknacks from a TV shopping-channel salesman who encouraged us to "CALL NOW, only two hundred miniature Elvis erasers left in stock." (*Sounds of the Seventies* on LP, I'll concede, is a must-have.)

Below are a few positive disciplines that can assist you in moments when you're financial putty:

1. **Keep your credit card frozen in a can.** I'm not kidding about this one. Take a coffee can, stick your credit card in it, add water, and FREEZE. If you really need it, you can thaw it out in a few minutes, but you'll feel awfully silly when you're frantically rubbing your ice-encased plastic under hot water so you can make the final two minutes of the "Pocket-Travel Gelatin Mold" TV offer. In my book, anything you can do to make yourself feel *silly or ridiculous* about buying something *silly or ridiculous* is a positive discipline.

2. **Find "no money" ways to get what you want.** I know this sounds simple, but this one habit has made a huge difference for me personally. Most of us made "getting what we want" synonymous with "opening our wallet." Instead of buying that home gym, find a friend who has one and workout together. You may both appreciate pairing up for a common interest. (Wouldn't that give you *even more* of what you *really* want?) Instead of buying new furniture, get creative and "antique" your old character-filled stuff. Rather than buying music CDs for one song you like (how many times have we done that?), find a local radio station that plays more cutting-edge stuff than you could ever purchase anyway. Get in the habit of asking yourself, "Is there a way to get what I really want without spending money?"

3. **Barter goods or services.** I do this a lot with sporting-goods equipment. In fact, there are retail stores that specialize in this kind of thing. Last year, I traded my Rollerblades in for a snowboard (asphalt bites). The year before, I found a guy who wanted my old laptop computer, so I traded him for a great camera and gear. Get in the habit of noticing the stuff you've "invested" money in that you aren't using. Then, pay attention to what your friends are seeking and ask them. Don't be a pack rat, especially if you're trying to get out of debt. You may have to wait a week or two for what you want, but (according to the above suggestions) you're going to do that anyway, aren't you?

4. **Don't get cash advances from your credit card.** Most of us go through cash in our pocket rather quickly, without retaining much to show for it. Borrowing money from credit card companies is expensive, and it's especially ridiculous to borrow money just for "walking-around cash." I know they make it easy, but don't do it.

■ EXERCISE:

Maintain a wish list. *Remember when you were a kid and you kept a meticulous birthday or holiday gift wish list? Same principle here. Find a place in your notebook and ANYTIME you find ANYTHING you even remotely want, write it down. It's a great habit to get into because you get to actually* feel *excited about the thing without shelling out the cash; it's also inspiring to have these material goals. Later, if you're still craving those Dura-Shears, you can get them. But a two-week waiting period has a real tendency to "weed out" impulse buys.*

To Do:

- Begin your wish list.

■ 5. UPDATE YOUR CREDIT HISTORY

The man who rolls up his sleeves seldom loses his shirt.

—Thomas Cowan

■ SCENARIO

Matt and Jenny were denied a department store credit card. Feeling like total losers, they crept out of the store under the cover of darkness, vowing never to leave the house again. Fortunately Jenny, who knew a few things about the game of credit, requested a copy of their credit reports (free, since she was rejected) and found several errors on each profile, none of which was the couple's fault. Once corrected, Matt and Jenny found the department store eager to extend them credit. (In fact, the store clerks, holding hands and singing "Kum Ba Yah," circled Matt and Jenny as the dewy-eyed couple spent a ton of dough on furniture.)

Here's how the credit game works:

There are three companies in America that keep credit history databases on CONSUMERS: *Experian (formerly TRW), Equifax,* and *Trans Union.*

When you apply for credit (card, mortgage, auto, etc.), the potential LENDER gets a copy of your credit history PROFILE from at least one of these three companies.

Your "personal" PROFILE, which has been filtered through risk-management software (like Emperica or Delphi), is assessed by the LENDER to make a judgment to either extend or deny credit to you.

Some things you should know:

When dealing with the credit-reporting services, each of which has historical data on 170 million CONSUMERS and processes 500 million reports per year, it is important to understand that you are **not their customer.** Their CUSTOMER is the LENDER. Get it?

You are the CONSUMER—one in 170 million. To deal with us pesky peon CONSUMERS, they rely on computers. *When was the last time a computer made a judgment in your favor?*

No one at big retailers or car dealerships gets fired if they say "no" to a borrower; they only get fired if they say "yes" and you turn out to be a bad risk. Credit managers live by one rule: **Cover Your Ass.** If you don't pay, they want to be able to tell their boss: "The Equifax profile was favorable. How was I supposed to know Matt and Jenny would turn out to be deadbeats?"

Starting to get the picture? Your credit profile should be as accurate as possible. Even minor errors or omissions can cause you to get computer-barfed. I was employed by Shearson Lehman Brothers for several years. Once, my credit report listed my employer as "Sherman Leasing" and "Shersing Lumber." That same report (TRW, incidentally) had my date of birth wrong (do I look twelve?) and my name misspelled. **It's never to your credit to have discrepancies between your report and the application you complete.** Unfortunately, the lenders will tend to believe their computers.

Q: What is on my credit report?

A: ■ Identifying information: *name, address, Social Security number, DOB, employer, phone numbers.*

■ Credit information: *a list of your accounts and payment history for major credit cards, department store cards, and other loan payments.*

■ Public record information: *bankruptcies, foreclosures, tax problems, etc.*

■ Inquiries: *Each potential lender's request is noted (multiple inquiries over a short period of time are frowned upon by lenders).*

Things NOT on your credit report: race, criminal record, religion, political preference, health, driving record, income, shoe size.

Q: Where do they get their information?

A: Retailers, banks, collection agencies, public records from courthouses— *anywhere they can legally dig up a financial bone.* Usually personal data, like your address and employer, they get from your application, so write neatly to avoid errors.

Q: Who can view my report?

A: Businesses, banks, creditors, collection agencies, insurers, and employers; anyone who has a "legitimate business need" to check into your creditworthiness. (As if that isn't enough nosiness, with your written permission or a court order, **anyone** can meddle in your credit report.) Oh yeah, YOU can see your own data.

Q: How long does my credit history remain on file?
A: Seven to ten years in most states. As low as five in New York.

Q: How do I get a copy of my credit report?
A: Ask. Pay. (Had to know that was coming.)

Call, write a letter, or go on-line requesting a copy of your **credit profile.** Make sure you include: full legal name, Social Security number, DOB, current and previous address, telephone number, payment (check or MO), and signature (credit card serves as authorization on the Net). Contact **all three** credit data companies:

Experian	Equivax	Trans Union
1-888-EXPERIAN (397-3742)	1-800-685-1111	1-800-851-2674
P.O. Box 2104	P.O. Box 74021	P.O. Box 390
Allen, TX 75013	Atlanta, GA 30374-0241	Springfield, PA 19064
www.experian.com	www.equifax.com	www.tuc.com

Turnaround time: 48 hours if charge by phone or www, four days by mail
Cost: $8 plus tax, SASE [less in CT, ME, MD, GA, VT—**FREE** if you've been denied credit, employment, rental housing, or insurance; are unemployed; are a fraud victim; are on welfare]

I'm not letting you off the hook on this one. CALL AND GET THE DAMN REPORT. Pretty please.

Once you get your reports, you'll want to do several things:

1. Carefully review every line of all three reports for accuracy. Report any errors immediately.
2. In writing, request notations attached to any items you feel need special explanation. You can add **up to 100 words** to any item. (**Tell your side of the story** if you were late on a payment because of illness, travel, unemployment, military call-up, medical bills, or change of address.)
3. Create a credit-report folder in your file, and update it yearly, at least.

To Do:

- Request your credit profile.
- Correct any errors; dispute and explain ambiguous items.
- Start a credit-report file, to be updated annually.

■ 6. KNOW YOUR CREDIT FILE RIGHTS

What is success in this world? I would say it consists of four simple things: to live a lot, to love a lot, to laugh a lot, and from it all, to learn a lot.

—Richard J. Needham

■ SCENARIO

Matt and Jenny get the picture now, and they're a bit teed off. Their credit report was not only a cold, intrusive little rag, but it was full of mistakes and had a misleading slant on their credit history. They've updated their report and have committed to keeping closer tabs on the credit data meddlers. Still, they wonder what rights they have. After all, they are the subject of these cold number- and code-strewn reports. It's their lives these reports are messing with.

As a consumer, you have certain rights regarding your credit and data. **You have the right to:**

Be considered for credit, insurance, employment, and other benefits on your own merits, based on your record of actions and performances.

Be treated with respect and fairness whenever information about you is used.

Privacy, consistent with the request and demands you make of business.

Have your applications for benefits or opportunities evaluated on the basis of relevant and accurate information.

Know what information has been provided about you for consumer-reporting purposes.

Know what customer data is being maintained about you and be able to review the information in reasonable time, at a charge that is not excessive, in a format that is understandable, and with the ability to challenge and correct inaccurate information.

Expect that information about you that is collected or stored for consumer-reporting purposes will not be used for unanticipated purposes without notice or consent appropriate to the circumstances.

Expect levels of accuracy consistent with sound practices or record-keeping and information systems management.

Have information about you safeguarded through secure storage, confidential handling within the organization, and careful transmittal to authorized and legitimate users.

If you didn't bother to read the list completely, I really don't blame you (but keep it for future reference). These "rights" are unbelievably vague and boring. They're a political speech and there's no real enforceable substance to them, it seems. But, hey, at least they **gave** us rights. I wonder how on earth they acquired these rights they're giving us in the first place. The point is: I'm telling you again, **you are not their customer.** Your creditor pays their bills. Get it?

Before I close, sounding like I despise their methods, let me offer the other side: one reason credit is so quick and easy to acquire these days is because of services like these. As a lender, you're more able to extend credit and make fast decisions with reliable information in hand. My gripe is that I think that the services don't send the report to the consumer first and let you hand it off to your potential lender. I've seen too many "confidential" credit reports lying around offices and faxed all over town to feel like there's a real interest in the consumer's "rights." Maybe it's not the reporting services' fault, but couldn't they at least notify us when someone digs into our file? (They do mail a "form letter" notice if you're denied credit, but to get the actual report you have to track them down.) Or perhaps, mail us a copy every year, without request, so we can check up on them . . . Not gonna happen, I'll bet.

Anyway, you and I aren't going to crush them, so just know that they are a powerful lot, and if you want credit, you have to play by their rules.

◼ 7. GIVE YOURSELF SOME CREDIT

There is enough in the world for everyone to have plenty, to live happily, and to be at peace with his neighbors.

—Harry S. Truman

◼ SCENARIO

Matt and Jenny have made their share of credit mistakes, but they understand the game now and want to begin building a strong credit history so they can buy a home and a new car.

Q: How do I build good credit history?

A: 1. Open a bank account (savings or checking) and use it responsibly.
   2. Apply for credit with a local retailer (or gas station) or take a small loan out at a bank.
   3. Make the payments on time and in full to begin your positive credit history.
   4. If you have utility services in your name (gas, phone, water, electricity), make sure you pay them on time and in full. (Don't leave them in your name if you move.)
   5. Apply for a credit card and pay the balance off each month.
   6. Don't overdraw your bank account.
   7. Seek help from a credit counselor.

Be aware:

1. People are frequently rejected because their application states that they haven't remained at one address for a lengthy time (usually one to two years).

2. People are frequently rejected because their application states that they haven't remained with one employer for a lengthy time (usually one to two years).
3. People are frequently rejected because their application states that they don't meet the minimum income requirement (which is not disclosed on their credit report).

■ 8. AVOID BUYING "PACKAGED EMOTIONS"

I have enough money to last me the rest of my life, unless I buy something.
—**Jackie Mason**

■ SCENARIO

Matt and Jenny are resolved to take control of their debt, credit, and spending. They've vowed to meticulously consider all major purchases, avoid their credit cards, and get their credit cleaned up. They're stronger than ever in their determination to take back control of their financial life.

Logically, we all desire complete control of our finances, but sometimes our "emotional buttons" get pushed, so much so that they override the most logical of plans and defenses.

Let me offer a bold but true statement from my experience: not many people who are working and middle class or above need ANYTHING. Most of us have a nice place to live, a decent car, good clothes, at least two TV sets, and plenty of food.

Q: How is it then that we're convinced to buy so much crap?
A: Because we're human. And human beings have emotional buttons that can be triggered without too much wizardry.

Think about it. Do car companies sell cars? Or do they sell speed, excitement, safety, and reliability? You know the answers. A car, to most Americans, is more than transportation from point A to point B. In some cases, our complete identity can be summarized by our driving preference. But, let me ask you a question: *who told us that a car was all these things?* (Watch the auto commercials on television, and you'll quickly get up to speed.)

The same advertising and marketing principles are used to sell virtually all luxury products.

1. They get our attention *(with a bold statement or eye-catching image)*;
2. create a need *(your old car isn't good enough)*;
3. push our buttons by adding some emotional value we desire *(who doesn't want to be sexy?)*;
4. and then they hook us by linking that emotion to their product *(if you buy car X, you'll be sexy)*.

What I am trying to communicate is that we need to be aware of the marketer's intent, and understand that they're damn good at what they do. They're so effective these days that they can sell us an emotion in a near-worthless product and we'll buy it. They're not above dirty tricks to make us drool over whatever it is they're peddling. They are masters of the psychological manipulation game. But we don't have to succumb. By understanding what's *really* going on in your head when the desire to acquire overcomes you, you can beat the urge to whip out your wallet.

As human beings, we've learned to make certain *tangible* associations in order to fulfill our *intangible* needs. We see that great **suit or dress** *(tangible)* and absolutely *need* it to **look good** *(intangible)* at this weekend's social event. We *need* that **StairMaster** in order to get **in shape.** (Did Rocky have a StairMaster?) Or need that latest **electronic gadget** in order to **be organized.** Many times we convince ourselves of these sometimes false associations—that material *wants* fulfill emotional *needs*—through our "internal dialogue." We see the suit or dress on the rack, project ourselves *handsomely* into it, and quickly make the judgment that the suit has made us feel *handsome.* Maybe we say to ourselves, internally, "Wow, I look great **in this**," or "They'll really notice me **in this.**" What we're really after is to **look great** or **get noticed,** and we're about to buy the tangible (suit) in an attempt to acquire the intangible (positive feelings). If left unchecked, this unconscious habit of attaching *material wants* to *emotional needs* can have a financially disastrous effect.

It may not seem like it, but this sort of "projecting" is a form of "negative internal dialogue." The unspoken implication is that without the suit "I won't look great" or won't "get noticed." At its root, this sort of negative internal dialogue stems from the feeling that "**I'm not enough** as I am." We falsely assume, **"I need (material object) in order to get (positive feeling)."** Does that make at least *some* sense, from your experience?

I think that this idea of buying the emotions we want is really a *self-esteem* issue, but that may be digging a little deep for this discussion—and for this author's expertise. I do believe, however, that there are certain "positive dialogue responses" we can adopt. Once practiced and internalized, these "responses" can assist us in making purchase decisions; now we're in control, deciding for ourselves whether the product in question is really going to fulfill our needs or not.

■ **EXERCISE:**

Before making any decision about a major purchase, answer the following questions in your notebook:

1. **"What do I *really* want from this product? What *emotional needs* do I believe this will fulfill?"** For example, "positive internal dialogue" regarding a new golf club purchase might be: "I think I may want new golf clubs in order to play better so I'll gain **respect** from my peers." (What you really want is **respect**.) Then, continuing: "Will that really give me the **respect** I'm seeking? Or is there a better way to get **respect** among my friends? Is it necessary to spend money in order to gain this **respect?**" Get the idea?

2. **"Do I *want* to afford this right now?"** Nobody likes to say, even to themselves, "I *can't* afford this.*" So a great piece of replacement dialogue is "I don't *want* to afford this right now." You can even use it aloud without feeling like a bum. It reminds us that we're being responsible and have considered other uses for the "economic power" in question.

3. **"If I *really* want this, don't I know where to find it?"** This question makes the assumption that you have yet to decide whether you *really* want the item or not. It implies that you are a smart consumer who's taking time to make a sound decision. Still, if you *really* do want it (after the two-week waiting period), you'll get it. You're not depriving yourself, you're just being smart.

4. **"I'd rather have . . ."** This is a great positive dialogue tool because it incorporates several of the concepts we've discussed. "I'd rather have . . ." forces you to think of *opportunity cost* and whether you might not prefer another thing of similar value. If you decide on product B, then you've not only made a sound comparison buy, you've actually fulfilled your heart's true desire by getting what you really wanted in the first place. Don't pooh-pooh the power of this little question, OK?

Remember, the whole idea behind these "positive dialogue responses" is not to deprive yourself, but to use them as tools to get what it is you *really* want.

But if you're in debt like most Americans, you need to pay particular attention to how and why you're overspending. There's a 100% chance, from my experience, that your buttons are being pushed quite frequently—maybe without your conscious awareness. If that's true for you, then the best defense is awareness. **Begin to view these advertisements through the eyes of a detective.** Notice their subtle (and not-so-subtle) imagery and try to uncover the "real" product they're selling. It's a lot of fun, plus it puts you back in the driver's seat.

But beware, even when you've caught on to them, their strategies tempt. Just last week I was watching a commercial for orange juice. It was clever, it caught my attention, made some stirring points, and hooked me. I'm telling you, I had walked to the fridge in a daze and was standing in front of the TV with a carton of OJ before I had even realized it. Before the commercial was even over I was chugging the stuff, unaware of what I was doing. That's crazy, but these images and messages are pounded into us deeper than we realize. So pay attention.

Before I close, let me rail for a moment with a specific example that could save you money:

A common mistake people make when purchasing electronics, appliances, or automobiles is buying repair insurance or **extended warranties.** (Their sales pitch is designed to push your buttons desiring **security.**) It's true that the extended warranty will pay the cost of repairing the item you buy after the manufacturer's warranty runs out, but it's also true that it is very rarely used; all it usually does is add to the dealer's profit at your expense. Here are more reasons extended warranties are a financial mistake:

1. If you finance the extended warranty, you'll pay interest and it won't take effect for years.
2. You pay for the warranty in advance even though it will not be in effect for some time.
3. You'll most likely sell, lose, or replace the item before the extended warranty kicks in.
4. It's a profit deal. Very little of the warranty monies are paid out in repairs. The rest is profit.
5. The salesman will love you (good feelings galore). This stuff carries big commissions.

To Do:

- Watch for "emotional" sales pitches or commercials.
- Begin using "positive dialogue responses" before any major purchases.
- Don't buy extended warranties.

Gone with the Wind:
Budgeting and Saving Strategies

Matt and Jenny struggle to save their beloved Tender and Greenbacks.

■

Annual income twenty pounds, annual expenditure nineteen six, result happiness. Annual income twenty pounds, annual expenditure twenty pounds ought and six, result misery.

—Charles Dickens,
David Copperfield

1. PAY YOURSELF FIRST: THE 10% SOLUTION

There are people who have money and people who are rich.

—Coco Chanel

SCENARIO

*Matt and Jenny are close to eliminating debt spending from their lives. They now have a budget, some sound financial habits, and a motivating goal: **to get out and stay out of debt**. But they don't want to forever settle for living at a financial sea level; they want to reach the summit. Getting flush is a worthwhile goal, and they're committed to giving it everything they've got, but they wonder how high they can really climb, what's really possible for them financially. Additionally, they've already begun to make plans for moving forward at a rapid pace. Their concerns, now, have to do with actually acquiring that elusive pinnacle called **wealth**.*

Hard fact: **in order to *have* money, you have to *keep* some;** you have to spend less than you earn. The statistics are amazing: **93%** of the families in America are still living from paycheck to paycheck. Most people seem to accept this deficit as inevitable; an income can only be stretched so far, after all. Contrary to what most people think, however, the paycheck-to-paycheck lifestyle is not a symptom of inadequate income; it is a symptom of inadequate wealth-building skills. Furthermore, they most always find that, as their income rises, there is no level of income they cannot outspend.

I'd like you to participate in a visual exercise for a moment: picture yourself standing in front of a cash register, about to make a purchase. In your pocket, you hold several green pieces of paper that represent a certain amount of **economic power.** Maybe these little green tokens of power have a kryptonic glow to them, and the "Twilight Zone" theme begins to play as you pull them from your pocket. Now picture yourself as you hand over this **economic power** to a clerk, who gives you some product in return; it's shiny, as well, but is not nearly as remarkable as the glowing economic power you gave in trade. So what's this about, you ask?

For starters, most of us tend to view products or purchases as something we **receive,** never really noticing the powerful, glowing object we **gave away** in exchange. We don't realize that the clerk is just as eager, if not more so, to make the trade. Why would they be so eager to barter such a shiny product they own? Because CASH IS KING, that's why. They know the value of a dollar; it's the consumer who has lost his money senses for the moment. They know they can buy more products, mark them up and sell them, make more money, provide more jobs, and build taller buildings with these little green glowing certificates of **economic power.** They understand "opportunity cost." So, they'll have sales and close-outs, offer you gift wrapping and free samples and coupons, and even advertise with sexy models in order to convince you to *give* them your **economic power.**

It's called "perceived value marketing"—you have to feel like you're *getting* more than you *gave,* which is rarely the case. They own vast numbers of retail outlets and buildings. You're still paying off your Pinto. Get the picture? It's never a fair trade. They know more than you. They don't want their crappy product; they want you to have it. Instead, **they want your money.**

So here's the point: **you hold tremendous power in your wallet.** If you use it, you can become rich. If not, they'll get richer. But, you've gotta understand that you're not just *getting* when you make these trades, you're also *giving* something powerful away: *your* precious **economic power.**

Let me drive this point home with a string of questions: *What do you remember about your last major purchase? Do you specifically recall writing the check? Or did you pay by credit card? Do you even remember signing the check or card? Or did you get so giddy you walked off and left your wallet/purse on the checkout counter? What was your state of mind in the moment? Were you deciding what shoes to wear with the new outfit? Were you even remotely considering what you were **trading?** Or were you only concerned about what you were **receiving?***

So, you've got to begin visualizing yourself "trading" your **economic power** for "stuff." You must picture what's leaving your possession, comprehending this interaction for what it really is: *a barter in which each party tries to make the most profitable swap.*

Now, let's take this a step further. (Stay with me here.) Instead of seeing yourself walking around bleeding out this **economic power** to whoever happens to be shaking a shiny cat toy in your face, picture yourself in control: you're walking through an outdoor market and the vendors start to dazzle you with sparkly trinkets, alluring scents, and compelling shell games and magic tricks, but you don't even stop. They yell their final "bargain" prices at you as a belly dancer, with their product tattooed on her butt, breaks into a wiggle. Still, you keep moving. You admire the gyrating belly-dancer a bit, eyeball their really neat gizmo, appreciating them both like fine art that you don't have to *own*. Then, instead of forking over a wad of bills in a trance, you wave politely, smile, wink (knowing their gig), and quietly move on. They wink back at you as you pass (you're now kindred in some way), and they turn their attention toward the next passerby.

Wouldn't it be great if, anytime you entered a retail store, you could notice the bright packaging and advertising tricks and relate that experience to the belly-dancer scene? How much more in control would you be of your **economic power?**

In order to accumulate wealth, **we have to save and invest a portion of our economic power.** You know that. So now, with these visualizing tools at your disposal—which you can use to shed some light on the manipulations you'll encounter as you struggle to hold on to some of your precious financial resource—let's get to the meat:

Each week or month, when you sit down to pay bills, you effectively divvy up your financial pie: a large piece goes for rent, another for auto and food expense, a sliver for utilities, and so on.

Now, I want you to picture yourself in front of this whole monetary pie, freshly baked and soon to be completely gone. OK. Now, the *very first* piece of that pie is cut and it goes **onto your plate.** Hang with me here. Before you even begin to decide who gets what piece, you're going to sneak *yourself* a small piece—about 10% of the total—and store it away for safekeeping. I'm talking about saving and investing, of course. Not rhubarb. (In that case, you'll want to scarf the whole thing.)

See, what happens to most of us is that we pay all of our obligations, buy a few things we want, then—if there's any "pie" left over—we save it for ourselves. But we've been so accustomed to seeing this "sharing" as a form of "keeping"—that is, we've been conditioned into believing that the products and services we "get" are good enough reciprocation—that we don't even consider ourselves as we slice up our economic pie. So, at the end of the month, we've paid the mortgage and the cable bill but kept nothing for ourselves: nothing "saved" to feed our hunger for wealth.

The sum of the wealth concept I'm goofily trying to illustrate is called PAY YOURSELF FIRST. It says that we must, must, must consider ourselves an **economic priority** and make ourselves the first beneficiary of our hard work. Again, buying things is not a *reward,* it's a *swap.* (Get that through your skull, please.)

The rule of thumb is 10%. Right off the top, **pay yourself first** *at least one-tenth of all your earnings and set it aside for investments, for building your wealth. If you have to,* **make yourself an invoice** (to you, for investments) and stack it on top of the pile of bills you're about to pay. That way, you won't forget to **pay yourself first** and you'll be constantly reminding yourself that you, too, are an important, deserving recipient of your **economic power.**

IMPORTANT POINT: No matter what your level of income, you can implement this strategy **today.** Don't fall into the trap of paying everyone else who'll lay a claim to your resources, thinking that you'll catch up (your savings) when you get caught up (your bills). It's a disastrous mistake that will ensure that you never, ever accumulate any savings. The only commitment that really matters, in the long run, is the one you make to yourself. You'll still be able to pay your bills. *After all, didn't they always get paid when you were earning even less income?*

■ 2. APPLY "TAKE-CHARGE" BUDGETING

Budgeting: a method of worrying before you spend instead of afterward.

—Anonymous

■ SCENARIO

Matt and Jenny don't believe they need a budget. After all, with rare exception, they only buy things they absolutely need. *Since there's not that much extra cash left over anyway, they justify, why hassle with a budget? Plus, the times they have considered a budget weren't particularly exciting, they recall. They feel that maintaining a budget is too time consuming, too boring, too depressing, and too confining. Consequently, they hardly even talk about it, except in a crisis. So on they go, making it month to month, hoping that things will be better, someday.*

Brace yourself, we're about to discuss the "B" word: BUDGETING. There. The ugly word's on the table, so get over it. If you want to experience the financial success you deserve, you're going to have to face one hard fact: **before we can move to the next level financially, we have to responsibly manage the resources we already control.**

If you are thinking of skipping this section, don't do it. There is a way to handle your finances wisely, thus preparing yourself for the next level, that's relatively painless. It's called "take-charge" budgeting and it goes somewhat against the grain of traditional thinking. Rather than requiring a tedious, strict spending plan (that you may not stick to anyway), the "take-charge" budgeting alternative focuses mainly on a few simple habits, which you can begin right away, that alter your "in-the-moment" spending awareness. You know *what* to do. The key to success is learning *how* to get yourself to do it. These "take-charge" habits, rather than demanding that you deprive yourself, actually allow you to have **more** of the things you want by encouraging you to simply *pay attention* to how you direct your economic power.

There are five steps to successful take-charge budgeting:

    I. Categorize your expenses.
    II. Determine your "real" spendable income.
    III. Set "control" spending amounts.
    IV. WRITE IT DOWN.
    V. Prioritize each expense as it arises.

In the next few pages, we'll dissect your spending patterns, define priorities, and begin to make "take-charge" budgeting a positive constant in your life. I think you'll find, as I did, that if you follow these take-charge steps, your goals will naturally follow.

I. Categorize Your Expenses

> *If it isn't the sheriff, it's the finance company. I've got more attachments on me than a vacuum cleaner.*
>
> **—John Barrymore**

■ SCENARIO
Matt and Jenny are willing to give an honest effort in order to take control of their spending. They've agreed to give budgeting a try, as long as it doesn't cause an argument—or give them a rash. Truth is, however, they don't know where to start. "Spend less" seems an appropriate command, but where? Where could they possibly cut down? What could they possibly cut out? They already feel they're quite disciplined. Where could they possibly find room to give?

The first step to any sort of change is **assessment:** *facing the reality of where you are now.* Categorizing your expenses is a quick activity that gets you in the mind-set of taking "spending inventory." This is not a judgment; it's just an honest peek into your spending portfolio.

■ EXERCISE:
From the list following, you'll mark each category that regularly applies to your spending patterns (a quick view of your checkbook register or bank statement will help). The idea is to begin seeing each purchase or expense actually falling into a *category. We're all familiar with rent or mortgage expenses, but where do maga-*

zine subscriptions fall? Perhaps BUSINESS or ENTERTAINMENT? Is that re-
cent airline ticket purchase for VACATION or BUSINESS? Are parking dues
under TRANSPORTATION or are they legitimate BUSINESS expenses?

    One of the habits I'm trying to encourage has to do with mentally DECID-
ING where you're spending your financial resources. Does the bulk of your
monthly income go to food? Doubtful. Clothing? No. Most likely, the bulk of your
monthly income goes toward housing and automobile expenses. So, the next ques-
tions you should be considering are: "Is there a way to reduce these 'fixed' expenses?
Are some of them business-related or tax-deductible?" That sort of habitual think-
ing and "paying attention" holds huge financial gains.

Expense Categories

_____	allowance/cash	_____	automobile
_____	business expense	_____	supplies (home or office)
_____	travel	_____	child care
_____	children	_____	clothing
_____	consumer debt	_____	contributions
_____	dry cleaning	_____	eating out
_____	entertainment	_____	family advancement (school, classes, etc.)
_____	gifts	_____	groceries
_____	health/fitness	_____	home repair/improvement
_____	insurance	_____	interest expense
_____	medical	_____	misc. expense
_____	mortgage	_____	personal
_____	pets	_____	publications
_____	rent	_____	savings/investment
_____	telephone	_____	transportation
_____	utilities	_____	vacation
_____	other: _____		
_____	other: _____		
_____	other: _____		
_____	other: _____		

    Categorizing your expenses allows you to "objectively" view your whole
spending map, which is powerful knowledge when plotting a forward course.
Remember, as the saying goes, *"The farther backward you look, the farther for-*
ward you are likely to see."

    So, do the exercise. It's easy. Just mark the categories you feel your spend-
ing falls under. Just do it, OK?

To Do:

- Quickly categorize your expenses.
- Practice mentally categorizing each expense as it arises.

II. Determine Your "Real" Spendable Income

Money isn't everything, as long as you have enough.

—Malcolm Forbes

■ SCENARIO

Matt and Jenny are starting to get the picture. Their incomes are relatively fixed, and they know those amounts to the penny, they think; it's their expenses that toss them the curveballs. They spend considerable time bringing in income, but very little monitoring how it goes out. Still, they believe, more income would probably do the trick; this dull budgeting work would be left behind if only their salaries would soar.

The single biggest mistake I see people make is in **thinking that more income will solve the problem.** That's false. If someone is mismanaging their resources at a modest level, their problems will only grow with their income level. Why do you think so many big-earning people in our society go broke? Usually, it's because they didn't develop sound habits early on, when their situation was manageable, so their money problems quickly leap over their heads. If someone can't keep a modest budget, are they really qualified to handle substantial sums? You know the answer. My point is this: **if you're starting small, you really are at a huge advantage**. You can practice and master good financial and budgeting skills while your situation is solidly within your grasp. Then, as *your skills* grow (which is really the only way your money situation will grow), you can begin to handle more and bigger finances.

An important step in "take-charge" budgeting is to determine your *"real" spendable income*. I know you know your salary, but that's **not** the number I'm talking about. That's not your *"real" spendable income*. Remember, you've already committed to a certain level of housing and auto expense; you've already been plunked into a certain tax bracket; and your employer already deducts moneys for medical and dental, Social Security, and other taxes. What's left over is your *"real" spendable income*.

■ **EXERCISE:**

So, let's just quickly knock it out. Our goal in this chapter is to come up with a pretty close "real" spendable income figure, which we'll use in later exercises.

First, calculate your total monthly income **after taxes and other deductions** *(or yearly "take home" salary and divide by twelve) and write it in the appropriate monthly box below. If your income varies month to month, or you are on a different pay schedule, it may help you to "smooth out," or average, your income in order to come up with a* monthly *number.*

Second, consider any additional sources of income, such as alimony, child support, outside ventures and royalties, and property income. Again, don't forget to subtract for taxes and deductions.

Finally, deduct your "fixed expenses," such as housing, auto, utilities, food, and clothing, to arrive at a total "real" spendable income *figure.*

	My monthly *income sources*	*My spouse's* monthly *income sources*
A. "TAKE HOME" INCOME (after taxes, deductions)	$_____	$_____
B. "INTEREST/DIVIDEND"	$_____	$_____
C. OTHER INCOME	$_____	$_____
Less		
D. "FIXED" EXPENSES (monthly total of housing, auto, etc.—anything "fixed" from month to month)	$_____	$_____
Equals		
E. "REAL" SPENDABLE INCOME	$_____	$_____

Please don't be discouraged by these figures. As we've already discussed, you most likely already have everything you really *need.* In fact, you'll find that you don't have to radically alter your lifestyle in order to succeed financially. You just have to "tweak" your habits a bit. Money success is not a huge undertaking, you simply have to maximize your existing economic power; over time, it's just that "slight edge" that will give you the biggest results.

III. Set "Control" Spending Amounts

I find all this money a considerable burden.

—**J. Paul Getty**

■ SCENARIO

Matt and Jenny are befuddled by this budgeting business. They've categorized their expenses, tallied up their income, while getting a healthy dose of reality in the process: their spending habits, needs, and wants bear no relationship to their actual income. They need housing, cars, clothes, and food, which make up the bulk of their monthly expenses. Now they wonder how they'll ever "squeeze" enough from their budget to save for a home and build some savings and net worth. Their "fixed" expenses are so high, and ever-constant, they don't see a way to cut them back dramatically—barring a granola-like lifestyle reduction (which ain't gonna happen).

Here's the good news: **it doesn't take that much to succeed;** a few positive habits can carry you a long way toward your goal.

Q: What would you do to become a millionaire?
A: *(you fill in the blank)*

Besides that. (Choose something exciting, noble, *and* legal.)

Most people can think of a lot of things they would do to become a millionaire, and most of these things are difficult or undesirable. *What If I told you that habitually controlling your expenses could make you a millionaire?* Would you do it? I would hope so, but the sad truth is most people won't even make this simple effort. With one minor adjustment (saving and investing), becoming a millionaire, over time, is as simple as getting control of your expenses and managing the excess wisely.

Let me show you an example: what if *every day* you took a George Washington (the dollar bill, not the quarter) and set it aside for savings, to build your net worth? I'm serious! Let's say you took a solitary buck, or the change in your pocket, and put it in a jar. (I don't know anyone who couldn't do *at least* that, do you?) So you've foregone a cup of coffee each day, and at the end of one month you've got a whopping thirty big ones, right? (Or thirty-one. Thirty days hath September . . . I'm confused.)

So far you think I've lost it, right? You're asking, "What could a dollar possibly do for me?" I'll show you. Let's say that at the end of each month you invested that money (I'll show you how later) and didn't touch it; you've set it aside for investment. With me so far?

The results of this little habit are truly astounding: **an eighteen-year-old who saves just one greenback a day is worth well over** *two million dollars* **at age sixty-five.** ($2,646,156.10, to be exact, assuming a 15% rate of return, which can be done.) Keep in mind that we're not talking about anything more difficult or time-consuming than, say, folding your underwear.

OK, so you're not eighteen anymore. What about five bucks a day, $150 a month? After twenty-five years, you've got just over **one million dollars**.

I can't repeat it often enough: **to be wealthy, all you have to do is learn to wisely manage the money that already flows through your hands.** Beginning to do this requires that you take a look at how you're presently allocating your resources, **discovering where you're trading your multimillion-dollar future.**

■ EXERCISE:

So, let's SET "CONTROL" SPENDING AMOUNTS by revisiting the list of your expense categories. Simply estimate your monthly expenditures by category and (again, your checkbook will provide valuable data) **write your monthly expense figures** *in your notebook.*

Expense Categories (monthly amounts)

_____ allowance/cash	_____ automobile
_____ business expense	_____ supplies (home or office)
_____ travel	_____ child care
_____ children	_____ clothing
_____ consumer debt	_____ contributions
_____ dry cleaning	_____ eating out
_____ entertainment	_____ family advancement (school, classes, etc.)
_____ gifts	_____ groceries
_____ health/fitness	_____ home repair/improvement
_____ insurance	_____ interest expense
_____ medical	_____ misc. expense
_____ mortgage	_____ personal
_____ pets	_____ publications
_____ rent	_____ savings/investment (10%)
_____ telephone	_____ transportation
_____ utilities	_____ vacation
_____ other: _____

You should be starting to see where your money is going on a monthly basis, which'll give you a good idea of where to begin with your savings, investment, and wealth-building programs.

IMPORTANT: finally, you'll want to "tinker" with the numbers a bit—take a few bucks from, say, CLOTHING and sneak it over into SAVINGS, formulating a visual idea of your new priorities. Again, these aren't set-in-stone spending limits, just "control" amounts. Don't balance them against your income to the penny just yet. (I'm telling you, strict budgets don't work. Most people tend to despise them horribly, then discard them after forty-five days, on average.) The idea is to simply "have a mental idea" of your spending matrix. Once you have a barometer of your spending disciplines, you'll find yourself looking for ways to "stick" to them.

Now you can relax a bit; the tough stuff is over. Next we'll discuss how you can use this "mental barometer" effectively, without depriving yourself and while having fun in the process. Again, don't make your "budget" too strict at this point. We don't want budgeting to become a "castor oil" academic exercise. Be cool. You know *what* to do. You'll make the necessary adjustments without cramming your head and wallet into a vise.

IV. Write It Down

What if everything is an illusion and nothing exists? In that case, I definitely overpaid for my carpet.

—Woody Allen

■ SCENARIO

Matt and Jenny, although very committed, are starting to feel maintaining a financial budget is going to be an all-consuming job. They feel as if they're going to have to "sweat the details" for years to come, noodling over every penny. Worse, they're concerned that a miserly lifestyle is what's required, which doesn't sound appealing in the least. Are they really going to have to pinch pennies and scrap over even the smallest expenses in order to make it?

One of the concepts I've learned about success that really, really works, and that needs to be in your vocabulary and foremost in your mind, is explained in one word: HABIT. Our health and diet habits shape our bodies and the length and quality of our lives; our time-management habits determine how we actually "spend" our lives; and our habits regarding people determine the depth of our relationships with family, friends, and associates.

Similarly, our money habits are at the core of our ability to build and maintain wealth, or not, throughout our lives.

What we want to do is create a positive habit that will help us stick to our budget without driving us crazy. Remember, one of the ways we develop habits, good or bad, is to *do the thing*. And one of the ways we make sure we continually *do the thing* is through conditioning (repetition and reinforcement) and immersion—adopting new skills and habits more effectively by throwing ourselves *fully* into the new endeavor, at least initially. Then, once the new skill has exhausted the need for our complete focus, we are free to relax a bit, while a more moderate, effective habit will stick with us.

Let me explain further with a personal example: I'm a runner now, but in the beginning it was tough to get myself outside consistently. (You might relate.) At first, however, I immersed myself in the sport by reading books and magazines, spending time talking with other runners, and—YES—"doing the thing." I actually began by training for a 10K (6.2 miles), which is not the simplest goal, and running *every day*. For nearly three months, I maintained this habit of running every day, stretching my distance almost weekly. (By the way, this does not mean you should go gung ho with regard to running. Take it slow or your body will never put up with the punishment long enough to become *conditioned*.) Anyway, after a few months I cut back to running two to three miles, three times a week, a habit I maintain to this day. Now what's key here is that my running habits now are **almost effortless.** I immersed myself in the sport to such a level that three miles, which is an awesome health habit, seems like a cinch today. I don't have to even think about it anymore. I just do it.

You can do the same thing with money. I want you to immerse yourself in its study, jump-starting the good habits.

One habit I call WRITE IT DOWN requires mild fanaticism at first. As the name implies, the trick is to habitually **write down every dollar you spend** in your notebook. In order to acquire this extremely positive discipline, you're going to have to go over the top and become absolutely nutty about doing it. EVERY DAY. ALWAYS. Eventually, the habit will take root and it will seem almost effortless as you go through your day; this awareness of where your money goes can give you tremendous control over your spending. If you're not yet convinced of the WRITE IT DOWN habit, consider this scenario: **You walk away from the cash machine with a stack of twenty-dollar bills, only to have it disappear without a trace. Where did it go? What do you have to show for it?** Sound familiar?

This used to happen to me all the time. I thought I knew where the money was going, but the truth is, I didn't. At times, I found myself being deprived of the things I truly wanted and deserved because I had spent a small fortune on things I couldn't trace and probably didn't really want.

What this WRITE IT DOWN habit does for you is truly mind-boggling; I wouldn't have believed it myself until I tried it and got results. Basically, it forces you to stop **quickly** and think about every purchase, its function and priority in your life, and allows you consider the long-term *opportunity cost* of such decisions, forcing you to stay mentally on top of your finances almost every waking minute. Now, I don't want to freak you out. You're not dwelling on money all the time, you're just allowing your spending to take up residence somewhere in the back of your mind. If you've ever been on a strict diet, where you had to journal constantly and count every calorie, you know what I mean. To this day, it's probably nearly impossible to consume anything without quickly thinking about its nutritional value. Make sense?

■ EXERCISE:

So, in your notebook, write down everything you buy, its use, its cost, the date, and where you bought it. *You'll be amazed at how your spending wants shift as you force yourself to log them.*

Are you really going to write down that you bought that dolphin back massager at the county fair? Is that really a priority? Does it really give you what you want? Or will you have forgotten about it in five minutes' time if you just walk away? *Those sorts of questions will automatically race through your mind as you make it a point to write your expenses down. More valuable is the fact that by considering your purchases thoroughly, you are now free to seek out and buy things you* really *desire. Think about it:* how many times have you told yourself "no" to something you really wanted, only to realize that you could have bought it had you just said no to the crap you didn't want?

The WRITE IT DOWN habit releases you from all that. *Voilà!* You're free. Enjoy your money.

To Do:

■ Write it down.
■ Enjoy your money.

V. Prioritize Each Expense as It Arises

You mean you can actually spend $70,000 at Woolworth's?
—**Bob Krasnow, commenting on the interior of Ike and Tina Turner's home**

■ SCENARIO

Matt and Jenny want to be responsible like anybody else. They also want their lives to be special. So, from time to time, they treat themselves to clothes or toys or a vacation every now and then. And they don't want that to change. Lately, however, they've been "scrimping" more than ever before; they needed to handle a few credit card payments that had gotten large, so they canceled their anniversary trip. They bought new tires, which meant they had to save that new stereo system until next year, and Matt needed a new computer, which came at the expense of . . . well, they're not really sure what that's costing them in opportunity yet.

There is a rule of life when it comes to having "things" that cost money. **It states that we can truly have *anything* we desire if we work for it, but we cannot have *everything*.** The first sign of financial maturity is to realize that there simply isn't enough money or time to have and do *everything* in the world. Life is short and things must be prioritized.

This step is designed to help you weed out the things that aren't priorities so you can **save and invest** (pay yourself first) as well as **spend time and money** on those things that offer the **most value** to your life. The best way to make these "prioritizing" decisions is as you go, at the point of purchase, when the money's spent. Whenever you make a purchase and record your expenditures, get in the habit of prioritizing right then; write an *A,B,C,* or *D* next to each item as you mentally make a judgment about its value. Use the following expense "priorities" and definitions as an example:

> A—NECESSARY (could be groceries, rent, gas, savings, etc.)
> B—IMPORTANT (could be clothes, gifts, health club dues, etc.)
> C—NICE (could be eating out, car detailing, trips, etc.)
> D—WORTHLESS (could be anything we buy on impulse.)

Again, once you condition this habit, you'll be making almost effortlessly decisions that can alter your financial destiny for the better. You know what "A" priorities (NECESSARY) are: food, rent, and so on. That's easy. "B" priorities (IMPORTANT) might represent the "comforts" of life: clothes, entertainment, etc. "C" priorities (NICE) get a little more difficult to define: vacations or toys, perhaps. And you already know what the "D" priorities

(WORTHLESS) are. You just know it in your gut when you've been hood-winked by a fairy-dust product such as trinkets or gizmos, sale items you just can't resist, or things you see in the checkout-stand line.

I'm not saying don't buy fun things. My point is that if you're not saving enough for your future or not fully enjoying your income—or especially if you're in debt—you can correct the problem by paying a little more attention to your expenses, especially your "D" priorities. So, please, give this little habit a try. Once ingrained, you'll be in great shape. You'll see that battery-operated neon necktie and think, "Cute little 'D' priority made for the suckers!" And you'll walk away laughing, in control and with cash in your pocket. Remember, **it's not what you earn, it's what you keep** that makes you wealthy. You can possess a closet of goofy neckties or you can be rich. Pick one. If you want to be wealthy, you're going to have to get used to making decisions like this.

To Do:

- Consistently prioritize your expenditures (A, B, C, D).

■ 3. SUMMARIZE MONTHLY

There are a million things in this universe you can have, and there are a million things you can't have. It's no fun facing that, but that's the way things are.
—Captain Kirk, "Star Trek"

■ SCENARIO

Matt and Jenny are "in sync" about their financial habits now. They've completed the exercises, formulated a strategy, and discussed it to the point of mutual agreement. They've both started carrying little notebooks and are WRITING IT DOWN and prioritizing like lunatics. They're ready to see their progress, to compare it from month to month.

Here's the complete and final budgeting drill:

- **Buy a specialized budget ledger** or notebook, with little squares for easy calculating.
- Set up sections for each of your **expense categories** (FOOD, TRAVEL, UTILITIES etc.).
- **Write in the budgeted *dollar* amounts** you are committed to maintaining for each category (i.e., ENTERTAINMENT, $300 monthly budget). HINT: you get the most benefit by allowing this budget to be a working document, revising and updating as your priorities change. Try one budget for a month and tinker with it. If you find $200 is enough for ENTERTAINMENT, then you can move the extra $100 to, say, SAVINGS (you had to know that was coming).
- **Get on a "posting" schedule** in which you take your daily expenses from your notebook and post them under the appropriate expense category in your budget ledger. HINT: I sometimes post them at the end

of each day, or week, and keep a running total (in pencil), so I am constantly aware of how close I am to my budgeted amount for the month. I can then adjust my budget or my spending habits to meet my budget.

FINAL TIP: for other tracking purposes, I always make a note in my daily expense form about the type of payment I made (American Express-AX, Personal check-CK, MasterCard-M/C, and so forth). Please note the optional column labeled "type" on your monthly budget organizer.

To Do:

- Buy a budget ledger.
- Set up your monthly budget sheet.
- Post your expenses regularly.

The Money Pit:
Effective Home-Buying Strategies

Matt and Jenny, seeking refuge from evil, swap all but their firstborn for a chronic lawn and a leaky roof.

■

Every man is the architect of his own fortune.

—Sallust, Roman historian and politician

■ 1. BUYING YOUR HOME: PLAN TO OWN AT LEAST ONE HOME

It should be remembered that the foundation of the social contract is property.
—**Jean-Jacques Rousseau**

■ SCENARIO

Matt and Jenny are ready to get on with the American dream; they want to buy a home. They're a bit perplexed, though, about what actually has to happen before they can start arranging furniture and mowing the lawn. First, they know, they have to find a house—although they're not sure how much they can afford. Next, they've heard that they'll need some cash for the down payment and closing costs, but they have no idea how much. Finally, they'll have to take out a mortgage, which is a process foreign to them at this point. So, adding all this up, Matt and Jenny aren't about to start packing yet. They'll just hang on, they figure, until all their home-buying pieces fall into place.

You already know that you're going to buy a home at some point, so start making plans now. It's easier than you might think, and it's never financially smart to toss rent money into the commode.

Buying a home, especially the first one, can be a big deal. There's new terminology to learn, some risk, and a whole new ball game to gear up for. But, in reality, buying a home is a smart move, well worth the time and commitment involved to make the move. Besides the pride of ownership, the roots of a neighborhood, the privacy, and the neighborhood barbecues, there are substantial financial reasons to own your own home:

1. Our government encourages home-ownership. Mortgage interest is tax deductible.

2. **Home ownership says you're stable.** Virtually everyone you do business with asks you on the new account application if you *rent* or *own*.

3. **Home ownership builds net worth.** For people who have trouble saving, a home (the largest investment most families ever make) is a kind of forced equity-building plan. Many people won't stick to a monthly investment plan, but they'll pay their mortgage every month without fail; after thirty years, they've accumulated substantial net worth because of their home.

◼ 2. BUYING YOUR HOME: KNOW YOUR HOME-BUYING RANGE

Wisdom is the conqueror of fortune.

—Juvenal

◼ SCENARIO

Matt and Jenny have been looking at new houses from time to time. They get excited visualizing themselves in a new home, but they aren't sure what they can or want to afford. The salespeople they've contacted will hardly even show them real estate without a firm price range, and the ones they do meet ask an endless stream of amicably intrusive questions about their jobs, income, and cash position. (Once, they "exaggerated" their price range—hey, who doesn't want to walk through Versailles?—and now they're barraged by even more inquisitive phone calls.)

The first thing you'll want to do when home shopping is determine your *real* buying range, saving time and disappointment by looking only at homes that you can realistically afford. If your budget's limited, you'll be looking at "cute" abodes. If you're a big-earner, you'll be seeing "exclusive" properties. And if you're Daddy Warbucks, you'll be checking out "estates." But no matter what your range, you'll feel the same sense of excitement that comes with the experience of home ownership.

Two major price considerations to keep in mind at this point:

1. **The down payment.** Usually 10–20% of the total purchase price; less for VHA and VA mortgage offers. According to the latest figures from Merrill Lynch, the cash needed to close on the average American home last year was around $28,000. If you can save $500 a month, and can

get a 12% return on that money, you should have the green in about four years.

2. **The monthly mortgage expense.** Usually not the biggest challenge because most of us are used to paying rent. It's the big cash outlay that knocks us for a loop.

■ **EXERCISE:**

They don't quote housing prices in "down payments" or "monthly mortgage payments," they quote them in "real" dollars—usually real BIG dollars—so here are some good rules of thumb for finding your home-buying range:

■ The home price should not exceed **two times your family income.**

■ **You should not pay more than 30–38% of income** (after federal income tax) for your monthly housing expenses (mortgage, utilities, maintenance, etc.).

Calculate these figures in your notebook, so you'll know where you stand from the outset.

◼ 3. BUYING YOUR HOME: DO YOUR HOMEWORK

Nothing is a waste of time if you use the experience wisely.

—Rodin

◼ SCENARIO

Matt and Jenny are jazzed. They've found their "buying range" and discovered that there are dozens of "perfect" homes that they could afford. Now they're puzzled over the many choices they'll have to make: Is that cute one under the freeway going to keep me up at nights? Will the one with the big lawn have a decent resale when they build that airport out back? Is the smaller one in the great neighborhood overpriced? And that big purple one that's been vacant for three years—what'll happen to that big ditch in the backyard when it rains?

A house is a huge investment—one of the biggest you'll ever make. So you'd better be sure it's a good one. But, hey, that's what I'm here for. Before getting enthusiastic enough to make an offer on one of your favorite locations, make sure you do some significant legwork into the details of the property and the area. Here are a few questions you'll want to remember to ask:

1. **Is there a decent school system nearby?** Certainly a decent question concerning your own kids, if you have them, but good schools help with the resale values down the road.

2. **Are there many houses for sale in the neighborhood?** If so, why is everybody leaving?

3. **Is there anything fundamentally wrong with the house?** Call the builder or the "previous-previous" owners of the property (the ones selling it to you will just rave).

4. **Why are the current occupants selling?** If the answer's vague, check the place out closely.

5. **What's it like to live around here?** Ask neighbors how they like the area and how long they've lived there. Are they nice people? Or do they have an unmistakable Jack the Ripper quality?

6. **Is the home reasonably priced for the area?** Again, ask your potential neighbors. Many are kind enough to tell you what houses in the neighborhood are selling for; they have a vested interest in the current property values.

7. **Is your realtor respected here?** Have your neighbors been hoodwinked by the same agent?

8. **Does it feel like home?** Can you see yourself happy in this environment? Are your neighbors near your age? Are there restaurants and shopping nearby? Is your place a favorite doggie-doo hideaway for the local pets?

Before you close, you'll have an inspector go through the house, so you don't have to dig around in the yard while the place is occupied. Still, you can ask some important questions without coming off like Columbo.

4. BUYING YOUR HOME: BE PREPARED
TO NEGOTIATE

The only successful negotiations are those in which everyone wins.

—**Jerry Nierenberg**

■ SCENARIO

Matt and Jenny have picked out a wonderful place. They've heard that "asking prices" are negotiable, but they don't know where to start. They don't want to look foolish or offend anybody, but they're determined to get that home for the best possible price. Matt recently purchased a Negotiation 101 *handbook and Jenny prides herself on her bargain-hunting abilities, so they're ready, they think. They plan on calling up the realtor, maybe playing a bit of hardball, and coming to terms in a few hours.*

You have to figure that your realtor, if they've been in the business a while, has done this sort of thing a million times. Before you even visited the property for the first time, they'd already sized you up, most likely on the car ride over. They have an idea of your income, your housing preference, and your buying range and time frame. They can sense if you're anxious to "get it over with" or if you're just "shopping" for good deals. (Telling them that your current lease is about to expire gives them even more ammo.) They are trained to "close deals" and, whether you know it or not, they've already plotted a course for your jugular. (Oh, and you're dead if your agent also represents the seller. Don't do that unless you're a real pro. So ask them first if they list the house.) By the way, keep your mouth shut during the "walk through."

Here's the deal: this home—the place you want to raise your kids and on whose front porch you wish to spend your golden years—now has a great *emotional* significance to you. They know that. You can't really hide it all that well, especially if it's your first home. But what you have to understand is that once you start the negotiations, all the warm-fuzzy stuff has to stop. Now you're making a business deal. And you'll never, ever feel good about over-paying for a home.

Two pieces of advice:

1. **Don't rush it.** You're about to make a big decision. The realtor wants to know, the sellers want to know, and the bank wants to know; everybody involved will be pushing you. But, remember: YOU HAVE THE POWER NOW. You are the buyer and the ball's in your court.

2. **Their tactics are shameless.** You'll hear all the lines as they whisper: "I hear they are really dying to sell this place and will seriously consider any offer," or "I'm showing it to another couple at 4:00. If you want to make an offer before then . . ." or "I've heard that interest rates are about to jump, so you'd better lock-in." (Top economists can't predict interest rate movements worth a damn. You're telling me a part-time realtor in Tulsa *knows?*) So just be prepared. The game has begun and you're the novice, so take your time and don't be suckered.

Here's a hypothetical scenario. (This actually happened to some people I know, but let's just assume it's you.)

Date	Time	Activity	Price
7/10		Noticed house with great view. Asking price:	$189,500
8/11		First visited house, noticed list price had dropped to:	$179,500
10/10		Noticed listing agents had changed, new asking price:	$169,500
11/8		Realtor said, "They'll entertain ANY and all offers."	
11/9		So, you made an offer on the property:	$119,500
		Note: sellers totally offended by offer,	
		but "want you to try again" at a higher level.	
		(You guess they weren't too mad to take more of our money)	
11/10		Saw more houses. Realtor hinted at "lowest possible price":	$149,500
11/15		You submitted a higher offer	$132,500
		(asking for the hot tub, washer and dryer and fridge, as well)	
11/15		Sellers counteroffered at:	$149,500
11/20		**Here's where things get hairy:**	
	3:30 P.M.	Realtor visited you and dropped off counteroffer:	$149,500
		You responded: "Take them our **final** offer:	$135,500
		No appliances—let them keep them. Don't come back with them	

wanting to throw in a microwave for an additional ten grand.
Call only if they say YES."

Realtor replies: "They won't take it. I know they won't take it."

**This gets you ticked off, because the realtor encouraged
ANY offer, remember?**

4:30 P.M.   You called agent, left voice mail: "You know, I think you're right.
If you're so sure they won't accept our offer, then why bother?
Let's just cancel our offer and drop the whole thing since
(again) you know for certain they'll just reject it."

5:30 P.M.   Realtor changed tune: "Well . . . let's at least take it to them."
(then rushed over to get signatures on offer)

11/22   12:15 P.M.   Realtor called, feigning enthusiasm: "You got a counter- $144,500
offer": You responded: "That was the final offer. If we go
higher, they'll just knock theirs down a nickel, or so. We're out."
Realtor replied: "Look, let's just meet in the middle."
You replied: "We're offering real money and they (sellers)
have been sitting on the house for a year. Now, if they were
to have countered at, say, $140,000, then we would be so close
we would have to take it." An unofficial figure is tossed in: $140,000

12:45 P.M.   Realtor: "Let's offer $140,000 then and see what they say."
You: "That's not what I said. Look, this guy has to win; to make
us **take** his counteroffer. We'll say $140,000 and he'll come
back with $143,399.50 or some such crap. If, by midnight, their
counteroffer were to read $140,000 (instead of $144,500),
then we'd take it, but the ball's in their court."

7:45 P.M.   Realtor calls: "You say $140,000. They say $144,500.
What if I cut my commission so we'd all meet in the middle?"
You: "Wait, wait. I'm not saying $140,000. Nobody's made that
offer. The offer was $135,500. The middle is $140,000. You're
inching me up again. Ridiculous. That's it. That's as high as
I'd ever go; on principle I would cut my finger off first."

8:15 P.M.   Realtor called: **"They'll take it."**
Property sold: $140,000

Remember the original list price of $189,500? It took a while, but you saved nearly **$50,000.** Now this was the rarest, toughest circumstance I could think of, but just because someone *wants* X amount doesn't mean you have to give it to them. I *want* world peace and a Lear jet, but . . . You also have to remember that if this weren't an acceptable price, the sellers wouldn't take it.

The whole idea of this example is to show you that negotiating is something you can't avoid. If the seller doesn't feel they scalped you, they won't be able to sleep at night because they wished their agent would have squeezed a few more bucks out of the deal. So be prepared for a negotiation. Even if the sellers and the buyers are reasonable and want to finish it quick, the realtors will still want to play their little games; it's their egos on the line now and they, too, want to feel like they've battled and won.

Of all the things you wear, your expression is the most important.

—Anonymous

■ SCENARIO

Matt and Jenny feel like outsiders when they talk to bankers and mortgage brokers. The bankers, although extremely friendly, respond very conservatively to their inquiries and are always tapping away at their computers in order to answer questions with exact *numbers—to the third decimal point. The mortgage brokers talk too fast, shuffle "ballpark" numbers around like crazy, and are always trying to get to the "bottom line." Matt and Jenny, intimidated, don't feel the bankers and lenders have even a remote interest in helping them acquire their dream home.*

First off, bankers and mortgage brokers, even though in this case they perform a similar function, are at different ends of the personality and professional spectrum.

BANKERS represent their bank and its related products and loans exclusively. They tend to remind me of Boy Scouts ("On my honor, to do my duty . . ."). They are very reliable, consistent, and responsible people. Every day, they take responsibility for huge amounts of money and are the kind of people you'd want watching over your most valuable possessions. Consequently, they never move very fast. "Getting in a rush," to them, is synonymous with "making mistakes," which they hate to do. However, their meticulous nature assures you that they'll know your balance to the penny, and their commitment and responsibility traits almost always mean they're squeaky-clean, honest, and loyal.

MORTGAGE BROKERS represent many different sources of mortgage funding, "brokering" money from a variety of sources,

many times nationwide. They are business people: traders and dealers. They pride themselves on being agile enough to take "prompt" action and are constantly looking for ways to increase their profitability. They talk fast, write fast, and make decisions quickly. They tend to remind me of car salesmen; their goal is to move merchandise, shake hands, smile, and sell you the most expensive hubcaps. But, they are efficient. The inherent nature of their business ensures that, if they have money to lend, they'll hustle to make a deal.

But here's what these two sets of professional people have in common: They have tremendous ACCESS TO MONEY. They're in the business of making loan deals. That's what they sell: money. They don't discriminate or exercise their personal values; they don't care. They just want to "sell" loans that won't come back to bite them and to get on to the next deal.

But—and this is a big BUT—both of these potential sources of financing are PEOPLE. They are concerned about making "bad" deals and losing their jobs. They have families and friends and have become used to people begging them for help. They've grown accustomed to being seen as powerful centers in their communities and are proud of the job they do. THEY ARE IN THE PEOPLE BUSINESS. All day long, they meet new people, schmooze a few, and console others. They have become good at sizing people up, and they have learned to categorize people. That is, they know with whom they want to deal—who's credible and reliable. They can also spot those who just waste their time and make them look bad. They will bend over backward for a good customer and condescendingly, yet politely, encourage a bad customer to look elsewhere. That's their job.

So, it's good business to understand the concept of RELATIONSHIPS. This one took me a while to learn, but it has proven to be so, so valuable. The idea behind maintaining business relationships is similar to that of family or friends. Over time, you become so familiar with one another that you share a certain "bond" that links you together, in good times and bad. You know you can count on each other and, in the earliest stages of any relationship, each commitment kept (or not) makes a statement about how highly you value that relationship. If your banker "knows" you well, and sees you as a valuable relationship asset, he'll be more apt to make certain considerations or exercise his power on your behalf. If he doesn't, or your relationship is strained, he'll be less likely to make substantial investments into the relationship.

I know this discussion may seem like it's a good distance from the concept of money and loans, but you have to understand that the **world transacts through relationships.** Foreign policy and politics are based on relationships. At work, you deal with relationships. At home, you nurture or neglect relationships. And if you want to borrow money, you'll need to develop long-term business relationships.

■ 6. FINANCING YOUR HOME: FIGURE OUT WHICH MORTGAGE TYPE IS BEST FOR YOU

Common sense is the knack of seeing things as they are, and doing things as they ought to be done.

—Calvin E. Stowe

■ SCENARIO

Matt and Jenny have started mortgage shopping but have found themselves on a confusing trail. Every lender they call wants to know "what kind" of mortgage they'll apply for: VA, FHA, or conventional? As sharp as they are, our couple quickly learned that "all of them" was not an acceptable answer. All they want to do is borrow money at the least possible cost (who doesn't?), but they are already stumped by the lingo.

When applying for a mortgage, you'll typically have three basic choices: FHA, VA, or conventional. And if conventional, you'll be lumped either into a conforming or nonconforming category. Normally all three programs will be offered by your potential lender, but you'll need to have already made a decision about which loan to apply for beforehand. If not, they'll sniff that you're a rookie and could be wasting their time, which you are.

First, a *mortgage loan* is simply **a loan made on a property that is pledged as collateral.** In the case of your home, the lendor technically owns the propery until you complete your mortgage contract, which is paying off the balance in full, plus the stated interest and costs. Now let's examine each type of mortgage category:

1. **FHA (Federal Housing Administration).** The FHA is a federal agency— within the U.S. Department of Housing and Urban Development

(HUD)—that assists in providing housing for **low- to moderate-income** families; generally, they don't provide the funds, but rather **insure** home mortgage loans made by mortgage bankers, savings and loans, and banks.

These loans are usually really good deals that offer lower rates and a lower than a 20% down payment (sometimes as low as 5% or 3% down), but they are designed for low- to moderate-income earners. Consequently, they have **maximum** loan amounts that your mortgage (including closing costs) will have to fall under. (Your banker will know the current numbers.) But for example, in the state of Texas, the maximum loan amount for a single-family residence (SFR) falls between *$86,317 and $135,375* (Texas is higher than the national average), depending on what county your property is in. FHA also offers programs for duplex, triplex, and fourplex purchases, with the maximum loan amounts slightly higher.

2. VA (Department of Veterans Affairs). Similar to the FHA, but *only* Veterans can qualify.

If you can qualify for a VA loan, it's usually the best choice because you'll be allowed to get in with **no down payment.** However, other closing costs may run $2,000, or more. Only those who have served twelve months or more of active duty in the armed services, and certain widows of servicemen, may qualify for a VA mortgage. The U.S. government sets the interest rates (which is really low) and rates fluctuate along with other interest rates.

3. Conventional. Any other mortgage that is not insured by FHA or VA.

With a conventional mortgage, rates are quoted in three basic down payment categories: 20%, 10% or 5% "down," which they'll quote as 80%, 90%, or 95% "financing." Be advised: **if you opt for a down payment of less than 20%, you'll have to pay private mortgage insurance,** also known as PMI; it's added to your mortgage amount and paid by you in monthly payments. Of course, interest is also paid on the insurance, so avoid PMI (by making at least a 20% down payment) if you can.

Also, once you've decided to go conventional, your lender will then shove you into one of two other categories, based on your credit rating and the size of the loan: conforming or nonconforming.

Conforming loans are those that are written on only the highest credit rated borrowers. They're always cheaper than nonconforming loans because you're less of a credit risk, which allows the paper to be easily sold to FNMA or FHLMC pools. The Federal National Mortgage Association (Fannie Mae) packages mortgages backed by the Federal Housing Administration and re-sells the pools to investors. The Federal Home Loan Mortgage Corporation (Freddie Mac) buys other qualifying mortgages from lenders, repackages them into pools, and sells them to investors on the open market. If you're la-beled nonconforming, then you'll be paying the highest rates and costs since your credit rating deems you a higher risk.

Once you have an idea of the loan you can qualify for, then you can really begin "comparison" shopping.

■ 7. FINANCING YOUR HOME: SHOP FOR THE BEST MORTGAGE DEAL

Energy and persistence conquer all things.

—Benjamin Franklin

■ SCENARIO

Matt and Jenny have called a few mortgage lenders and asked for their "best rate." They've also met with a few mortgage brokers and discovered that there was more to the process than just getting the best rate. First, they found out that the best rate quoted over the phone hardly ever applied to them; it was a "door swing" designed to get them to make an appointment. Second, they realized that every lender has their own unique way of quoting costs and fees, so comparison shopping has been difficult at best. Finally, they have become so frustrated by the whole process that they're now wary of all lenders; they can't tell who's trustworthy and who's not.

Mortgage shopping is a difficult process. Most people find that they are unfamiliar with the lingo and have no idea how to contain all the variables and "hidden" costs that lenders tend to tack on—a great disadvantage, especially since they shop only every few years; the mortgage bankers do this every day.

After you've obtained a listing of lenders in your area (your realtor should have access to names and numbers), you then have to do a bit of homework so you can compare "apples to apples."

There are four basic areas you'll need to be familiar with: *rates, points (or fees), closing costs, and loan program (or terms)*. Let's tackle each area one by one:

1. Rates. Usually the easiest comparison, the rate is the percentage finance charge you'll pay on the mortgage amount borrowed. Once you know exactly what program you want (see sections following), then you can simply choose the lowest rate among them. Be advised, however, that most conforming loans are offered at about the same *rate;* it's the *points or fees* that are the most variable.

2. **Points (or fees).** To process your loan, the bank or other lender tacks on their profit incentive: points. They may also call this an *origination fee* or a *lender fee.* Either way, it's money out of your pocket into theirs; it is not a part of the borrowed amount, but immediate income to the bank. A one percent origination fee is common, but they'll sometimes charge more (perhaps offering you a lower rate as an incentive); sometimes they'll charge less (offering a higher rate to compensate). The highest origination fees are charged by mortgage brokers, rather than banks.

3. **Closing costs.** This will probably amount to several thousand dollars either way you slice it, and you can't finance these costs; they must be paid at closing. These closing costs are usually negotiable and can be broken down into three separate categories, for comparison: *lender fees, settlement agent/title company fees, prepaid items.* By category, here's a list of common closing costs:

■ **Lender fees.** These are paid to the mortgage company or bank and can alter your "effective" rate dramatically.

$225–$500   Appraisal Fee
Appraisals are done by independent appraisers but are ordered by the mortgage company. If you find an appraiser who offers reasonable rates, request that the bank use *them;* they usually will if *your* appraiser is on their "approved" list, and you may even get a copy of the list to call from.

$45–$100   Credit Report
Some lenders will pull your report for free, before they've earned your business, and eat the charge themselves.

$100–$500   Miscellaneous Lender Charges, Document Fee
Look out for these. They're often called by names such as underwriting, processing fee, document preparation, courier, loan submission fee, wire transfer fee, lock-in fee, etc. This "junk fee" list isn't complete because lenders make up new names every day. If they know you're onto them, they may knock most of them out, so ASK.

■ **Settlement agent/title company fees.** These fees are not controlled by the lender, but by a separate title company that you, as the consumer, have the right to choose. (So call first and request a list of their costs.) The fees paid to the settlement/title company vary by state and company, but often include the following **estimated** costs:

Title insurance	$2.50 per $1000 borrowed
Survey	$100–$200
Attorney/closing fee	$250–450
Pest inspection	$15–$35
Transfer tax	Varies
Recording fees	Varies
Title search	$150– $350

■ **Prepaid items.** Borrowers are required to prepay certain items and put taxes and insurance in escrow; usually these industry standard costs do not vary much between lenders. They include:

Two months real estate tax (held in escrow)
One year homeowners insurance (paid at closing), which your lender requires. (What if the place goes up in smoke and you walk away? They've thought of that.)
Two more months' homeowner's insurance (held in escrow, to assure funds so the insurance doesn't lapse because of late or nonpayment)
Interim interest (on just about everything)

The best way to avoid getting hung out to dry is to know what's going on. Call each party involved and ask them to quote their complete costs. They'll still surprise you with "just one other thing," rest assured, but you can eliminate most of the unnecessary expense by being informed.

4. **Loan program (or terms).** This will be your biggest long-term mortgage decision. The most common loan program is the thirty-year fixed, but there are many other options available that may work better for you. Below are just a few.

Thirty-Year Fixed	As it states, the terms of the loan remain fixed for the period, thirty years.
Strengths:	Long-term rate security

Drawbacks:	Often the highest rate; may be more rate security than you'll ever need.
Tips:	Great if you don't plan to move or refinance for ten years, or more. (Average borrower stays in their home about four and a half years)
Fifteen-Year Fixed	As it states, the terms of the loan remain fixed for the period, fifteen years.
Strengths:	Fifteen-year rate security; more of your payment goes to principal; less to interest.
Drawbacks:	You may qualify for smaller loan amount than for the thirty-year programs.
Tips:	If you can afford it, even though the payments aren't nearly double, this is a great way to go. You'll build more equity, pay off in half the time, and pay less in interest charges.
3/1 Adjustable	(thirty-year amortization). "Adjustables" have rates that change every so often, throughout the life of the mortgage. On the **3/1** adjustable, the rate is *fixed* for **three** years, then *adjusts* every **one** year (based on the one-year Treasury, plus some other interest add-on). A cap (of 5–7% additionally, for example) ensures that your rate will never go higher than a certain level.
Strengths:	Lowest qualifying; allows borrower to "qualify" for largest loan.
Drawbacks:	Three-year fixed may not be enough rate security.
Tips:	Fine program if you believe rates will lower after three years or plan to move in three to five years.
	1 year adjustable, 5/1 adjustable, and 7/1 adjustable are available as well.

It's a good idea to keep a "matrix" or log in your notebook of each type of loan you're considering. Make four columns (for *rates, points, closing costs,* and *program*), so you can compare "apples to apples."

To Do:

■ Shop for the best mortgage.
■ Compare "apples to apples" by keeping a log on each program your lender offers.

■ 8. FINANCING YOUR HOME: DON'T TAKE "NO" FOR AN ANSWER

Never give in, never give in, never, never, never, never, in nothing great or small, large or petty . . . never give in.

—Winston Churchill

■ SCENARIO

Matt and Jenny completed their mortgage application then happily went shopping for new furniture. Long story short, their application was denied and their new furniture is now parked in their garage.

If you've been denied credit, especially for a mortgage, there are several steps you should take:

- ■ Get the reason for the rejection, in writing if possible.
- ■ Correct any errors on your credit file or application.
- ■ Determine if there is a better way to disclose the information on your application. Ask the lender if there was any information that could be stated differently, or what *specific* areas triggered the rejection.
- ■ Then, with your newly acquired experience, try again. Lenders' requirements vary and you may have just found one that didn't suit your needs. Also, banks vary on the amounts and types of mortgage money they have available; if they're *short*, they won't be too eager to assist. If they're *long*, they'll try to make it work. When you apply again, let your new lender know that you've already tried, but didn't complete the application accurately, if that's the case. Then, ask for their assistance; they know the game.

If you've had a mortgage application turned down, or if you have an unusual mortgage situation, it's possible mortgage brokers may be able to help you. So contact them, explain your situation in detail and ask if they think they can help you. Contact several brokers if necessary; you may have to pay more in costs or interest expense by dealing with them (as opposed to banks), but chances are you can get the loan you're after.

■ 9. FINANCING YOUR HOME: CONSIDER A FIFTEEN-YEAR MORTGAGE

Money is better than poverty, if only for financial reasons.

—Woody Allen

■ SCENARIO

Matt and Jenny have determined that they could afford a fifteen-year mortgage if they wanted to. They know the payments will be a bit higher but are considering just biting the bullet in order to save themselves thousands in mortgage interest. If they knew how much savings they were talking about, however, they'd be in a better decision-making position.

Here's a quick way to compare the charges of a thirty-year fixed versus a fifteen-year fixed mortgage:

Take your **monthly payments** for each and **multiply times twelve** (months), then **times thirty** (years), then **fifteen** (years), and compare. The difference between the two is "extra interest."

For example:

LOAN AMOUNT	MONTHLY PAYMENT		TOTAL PAYMENTS	
(@ 9% INTEREST)	30-YR. FIXED	15-YR. FIXED	30-YR. FIXED	15-YR. FIXED
$150,000	$1206.93	$1521.39	$434,494.80	$273,850.20
			The difference:	**$160,644.60**

In this example, you could save more than **$160,000** in pure interest by taking out a fifteen-year mortgage instead of the thirty-year. The payment differential of roughly three hundred a month makes this an extremely compelling consideration if you can qualify for it.

If not, you can still get nearly the same effect by taking out a thirty-year mortgage and making **extra payments** equal to that of a fifteen-year amortization. Neat, huh?

10. FINANCING YOUR HOME: USE THE 2% REFINANCING RULE

There is no security in this life. There is only opportunity.

—**Douglas MacArthur**

■ SCENARIO

Matt and Jenny want to consider refinancing their home sometime down the road, if rates drop enough to make it worth their while.

"Refinancing" means taking out a new mortgage on your existing property, which pays off the previous loan, hopefully saving you money because the "new" interest rate is lower.

The 2% rule is just a "guesstimate" about when it becomes profitable to refinance your existing mortgage. Because of the aforementioned loan origination expenses and costs, if the current rate you can qualify for is at least 2% lower than your existing mortgage rate, it may be wise to refinance.

You'll have to jump through all the same hoops you did during your first financing application, but it could save you thousands in interest by "locking-in" the lower rate.

Nine to Five:
Making the Most of Employee Benefits and
Retirement Plans

Matt, golden-handcuffed to his desk, struggles violently to milk the system.

■

If you're working solely for the paycheck, no matter how many zeros it has on it, you're still at a subsistence level.
—**Jack Nicholson**

■ 1. TAKE A LOOK AHEAD

Dare to be what you are and believe in your own individuality.
—Henri Amiel, Swiss poet and philosopher

■ SCENARIO

Matt and Jenny both have great jobs that they enjoy. They're paid reasonably well, they get along fine with their co-workers, and they are committed enough to work long hours. Additionally, both of their positions offer substantial benefits, such as health and dental insurance, retirement programs, training, and opportunities for advancement. Consequently, they've not given much thought to their long-term employment future; their situation seems just fine as it is.

But it is time to look ahead; financial realities force us to think about retirement from the moment we begin working. This time of reflection on the future offers a valuable opportunity to take inventory of our goals and working lives.

Many people are fortunate enough to find themselves in the "perfect" employment situation. Many others, however, are simply stuck in a comfortable rut and are too frightened to make a change; even if it's less than ideal, **the *known* seems better than the *unknown*** opportunities that may exist elsewhere.

Here's a great way to ensure you're making the right *daily* decision about your present employment situation: consider a few of your superiors or other mentors who have been with your company for a number of years, and ask yourself these questions:

1. **Do they seem fulfilled in their positions?** Pay close attention because, over time, this is where you're headed. You'll eventually become a "superior" or mentor in your company.

2. **Do they work as hard, or harder, than you do?** Again, their stamina reflects the company's expectations. If you want to eventually slow down a bit, and your superiors still plow ahead, then look out.

3. **Do you desire to become like them?** Conformity happens gradually. Whether we are aware of it, or not, we eventually become just like the people who surround us.

4. **Are their positions and levels of fulfillment high enough to meet your expectations?** It is unlikely that you will substantially alter the organization during your career. Is there enough potential present? Do they allow "superstar" performers? Or is that sort of distinction frowned upon?

5. **Do your company's values mesh closely with your own?** If every day is a battle to get them to see things your way, be prepared for a future of disappointment and struggle.

6. **Are they as committed to you as you are to them?** Unfortunately in today's environment of downsizing and layoffs, many people find themselves highly trained in extremely specialized areas of their company's business, over time. Consequently, they've pigeonholed themselves in the event they were to be "right-sized" or simply replaced.

7. **Do they swap management or bosses on you frequently?** This is a good indication of how they value their employees and *you*. Management changes are sometimes designed to "shake up" the workforce; they'll keep you on your toes to milk your best output. Make sure you have a clear understanding whether they want frenzied "short-term" output from you, rather than "long-term" growth and loyalty.

8. **Does your company really offer the potential financial rewards you desire?** You're probably not ever going to make more than your boss, and most certainly not more than the president of the organization. Is that potential enough for you?

9. **Does your company encourage input and ideas from employees?** Make sure they don't just *talk* about teamwork. If the power is solely concentrated at the top, you have to ask yourself how much value they really place other members of their "team."

10. **Do you like them?** Simple question, right? Are these people the ones you want to spend forty years working with?

11. **Have they changed over the course of their career?** Has your one-time creative, inspiring boss become just another cog in the corporate wheel? If so, chances are you'll face the same pressure at some point.

12. **Is your "expected" career path really where you want to go?** Sometimes we get "labeled" by our first position in the company and aren't able to "crossover" to more rewarding areas. Make sure you're not falling prey to a cold organizational chart.

The whole point is to force yourself to consider where you're *really* going. Is it still consistent with what you signed on for? As human beings, we have an inherent distaste for change—even when it's best. In the daily fight to pay our bills and do what's expected of us, we tend to overlook the idea that our skills might be better harnessed in another direction. Who can worry about their destiny when you're scrambling to make deadlines and quotas?

Look back in your notebook at your definition of success and your purpose statement. Are you meeting your own standards day by day?

■ **EXERCISE:**

Pull out your top ten highest life values, then compare the big five to those imposed upon you at work.

For example:

MY TOP FIVE LIFE VALUES	MY COMPANY'S HIGHEST VALUES
1) Health	1) Promptness
2) Relationships	2) Teamwork
3) Fulfillment	3) Communication
4) Challenge	4) Profitability
5) Sense of purpose	5) Commitment

The above comparison makes for a pretty good fit, professionally speaking. These "personal" values are nearly dead on with the company's "professional" values; which lays the groundwork for long, rewarding career potential.

On the other hand, if you highly value *creativity* and *progressiveness*, and your company highly values, say, *tradition* and *organizational systems*, look out. You're in for an uphill battle because your "right-thinking" values will inevitably clash with theirs. You'll be constantly trying to prove your point and progress in the way you think is best—through your ideas, work priorities, presentations, and communication efforts. And they'll be constantly trying to make you a "team player" by imposing their rules for success upon you. But nobody's wrong here. Values aren't right or wrong, just different, even though we all tend to adopt the idea that our way of living and thinking is "right."

Here's the problem with a personal and professional "clash" of values: your employer is constantly weeding out workers that don't fit into their "mold," which is a "proper" organizational procedure. If you've ever built or been a part of a successful organization, you know that there's tremendous power in heading a large crew in the same direction. On the other hand, a "misdirected" collection of individuals will eventually destroy the company by pulling it into too many different directions. Consequently, employers aren't too excited about "changing" direction too quickly, and they probably shouldn't be. As well, they aren't too interested in "molding" their workers into their mind-set either. They've found that it's more effective to simply "search out" people who already exhibit the values they believe are consistent with their own; they've also learned to quickly "weed out" those who aren't tracking the same course, either by neglect (no training or promotions) or outright replacement.

It's a tough situation to be in, for you and for them. Remember, the achievement of their goals and plans requires employees that push forward in that predetermined direction. You don't want to be seen as a hindrance or a barrier to their mission, even if you know you're "right."

Take a moment to list your TOP FIVE HIGHEST PERSONAL VALUES and compare them to what you perceive is your COMPANY'S TOP HIGHEST VALUES. (HINT: Some companies will have a mission statement that may include their highest values.)

MY VALUES   **"OUR" COMPANY'S VALUES**

1)
2)
3)
4)
5)

So how do these two lists compare? Is the company's mission statement consistent with your desires, but their social norms something entirely different? Are you their golden boy or girl? Or do they perceive you as a loose cannon that could redirect or stall their efforts? Do you still think you can change them?

The whole idea is to make absolutely sure you're in the right place. If not, you'll find yourself unhappy and deflated in a few years; without the financial success you deserve. If you don't feel appreciated or important at your place of business, chances are, you're probably not. They may not need or even understand your unique skills and gifts. If that's the case, you better move on—quickly. The big bucks aren't going to be showered your way if you're not "one of them." Is that harsh to consider? You bet. Unfortunately, it's a harsh world sometimes. Don't knock yourself down before you've had a real chance to shine.

By taking this "look ahead" you can save yourself years of constant "small" disappointments. On the other side of the coin, if you find yourself in the "perfect" situation, then do your darnedest to appreciate it. Work your tail off, be a team player, and be loyal to your co-workers and employer. Many people have grown wealthy and happy by being a part of a winning team.

Many of us make long-lasting career decisions at an early age and at pressing times—say, as soon as we graduate and need the money. When we take our first jobs, most of us are young, and lack the experience necessary to make a sound, long-term decision.

There's no way we could, really. We haven't had the benefit of years in different career paths and positions. Consequently, many people find themselves "trapped" before they've even had a chance to look at the menu. It takes guts, I'll agree, but believe in yourself. There really is a career path out there just for you. You may even have to design it, but everyone has a niche and we're all valuable enough to make a good living by pursuing our unique vision. Oh, by the way, that's where the big bucks are anyway.

2. UNCOVER YOUR RETIREMENT INCOME SOURCES

The highest of all possessions is self-help.

—Thomas Carlyle

■ SCENARIO

Matt and Jenny are pretty happy with their current employment situations. If all goes well, they might not mind retiring from these companies some day. It's a long way away, but they know they should start making plans for retirement now and taking advantage of the benefits they have been offered at work. Besides, even if they do change companies down the road, they know they'll be better off having maximized the opportunities their current employers offer.

Most of us wait until it's too late to plan for retirement. Retirement planning is so much less taxing if we get on it early, and I mean that literally. This is an important, cost-effective way to save. Here's a preview of your retirement income sources:

1. **Social Security.** Not as much as you might think. Only about one-fourth of your income during retirement will come from the government. The rest had better be in your investment and retirement accounts.

2. **Your company retirement plan.** Usually the best way to sock away big bucks to eventually draw on for retirement income. They usually offer "direct deductions" from your paycheck (which come out before taxes and usually compound tax-free until you retire), and most employers offer you reasonable investment choices.

3. **Your personal retirement plan.** This is what separates the wealthy from those who just scrape by in their later years. Once you max out your company's plan, you'll want to focus on other tax-deductible and tax-deferred vehicles for your savings, like IRAs and Keoghs.

4. **Your savings and investments.** If you want to be really, really wealthy, you're going to need "other" assets besides those that fall into "retirement savings" categories. Our government wants you to save for your future, which puts less burden on Social Security, so they do offer tax breaks for diligent savers. However, such plans are subject to a set maximum contribution and, for most people, only assure a standard of living similar to that of the working years.

A good rule of thumb is that you'll need about **70–80% of your present income** for your retirement, more if you have exotic plans.

■ 3. ASK SMART RETIREMENT-PLANNING QUESTIONS

He that lives upon hope alone will die fasting.

■ SCENARIO

Matt and Jenny are eager to get an early jump on retirement. They know that planning ahead is the surest way to make the most of their retirement years. They also realize that no future is completely predictable, so they want to get busy planning and overcome any unforeseen obstacles as they arise. By planning early, and having time and a sound plan working for them, they'll be flexible enough to weather any potential storms that would otherwise upset their plans for an enjoyable retirement future.

Having an adequate retirement plan is the most effective way to reach your long-term goals. When changes or obstacles arise, as they most always do, you will have your plans and goals to fall back on; to redirect you back on course. The biggest mistake I see people make in this area is that they plan for everything to go "perfectly." They run the numbers and *only* do what is necessary to achieve their goals, not a lick more. Which is a big problem if the financial markets or the tax laws don't cooperate. (You'd be surprised at how often these disappointments really occur.) If you begin planning for retirement early enough, though, you can overcome a wrench or two being thrown into your plan and still reach your destination with room to spare.

To begin, you'll need to ask yourself a few smart retirement-planning questions. Your answers will set the foundation for your goals, plans, and actions. However, not getting a good handle on your future needs and desires will offer mediocre results, at best.

■ **EXERCISE:**

Here are **Smart Retirement-Planning Questions** *you should answer in your notebook:*

1. **When do I want to retire?** Pick a date, an age, or at least a range of years that you would like to retire. This goal will give you the "starting point" to work backward from.

2. **How much income will I need at retirement?** Would you like to have the same lifestyle you have now? Or better? Remember to consider "today's dollars" as only a "relative" figure because inflation will erode your purchasing power at least 5% per year (i.e., in thirty years, you'll need nearly $9,000 for every $2,000 in today's income dollars).

3. **What sources of income do I expect to have?** Should be at least the standard four: Social Security, company retirement plan or pension, personal retirement plan (probably an IRA), and personal savings and investment assets. Calculate what each of these may be worth on your day of retirement. Is that enough? Or do you need to save more or invest more profitably?

4. **How much, in personal assets, will I need to accumulate?** This is where it gets a bit tricky. If you're planning on retiring in, say, thirty years, then you'll need to have a "liquid" asset worth of about **fifty times your current annual income,** considering inflation and the growth of your savings assets. That's a huge number, I know, but remember that we're dealing with the future; things will cost more, plus your net worth will be accumulating growth and interest over that time, as well. At retirement time, you'll want to "draw down" only about 10% of your "liquid" asset base per year. Considering the interest and growth you'll be receiving from your investments, you'll only actually "erode" your nest egg at the rate of about 4% per year; which gives you nearly thirty years before you run out of retirement cabbage.

5. **How much can I save each year or month?** From most of the studies conducted in the financial industry, a young couple saving 10% of their income will easily reach their retirement goals. So start there: **save one-tenth of everything you make and invest it.** After thirty years, you should have accumulated about fifty to sixty times your average annual salary, assuming you invest and achieve a rate of return of, say, 11% per year, which is about what the majority of stock-based mutual funds have historically given.

Q: What if I'm confused by all this running-the-numbers business?
A: Use the estimate *Rule of 72*.

There is a practical, simple tool you can use that roughly answers the question: *how long will it take for my money to double?* It is a great tool if you want to avoid exact calculations. Here's the rule:

To find **how long it will take for your money to double at various rates of return,** simply:

DIVIDE **72** BY THE RETURN YOU ANTICIPATE RECEIVING.

For example:

At an annual return *rate* of	your money will *double* every	
10%		7.2 years
7.2%		10 years
8%		9 years
12%		6 years

Get it? *The Rule of 72* can be a valuable approximating tool if you remember two things:

1. It's a "straight-line" mathematical calculation and doesn't consider taxes or other variables.
2. It only works on "lump sum" amounts for calculation, not monthly savings contributions.

At some point, you're going to have to become familiar with using a financial calculator or rely on an expert for assistance.

Lastly, keep the above questions and answers in your success notebook; they'll become valuable as you begin specifically planning your retirement future.

To Do:

■ Answer the Smart Retirement-Planning Questions in your notebook.
■ Approximate your saving potential using the *Rule of 72*.

■ 4. GET TO KNOW YOUR COMPANY'S RETIREMENT PROGRAM

Before you invest—investigate.

—Salmon P. Halle

■ SCENARIO

Matt and Jenny both work for established companies that offer excellent retirement programs. Still, they'd like to be sure they're making the right decision to participate at certain levels. So, they've decided to learn all they can about tax-deductible and tax-deferred retirement programs. That way, they'll feel confident about their own decisions. Besides, they need a new activity to spice up their Friday nights.

It's easy to be confused by the different types of retirement plans available, so here's a primer on the four major types of plans offered by employers and funded through payroll deductions. From the list below, determine which type of program is available to you.

1. 401(k)—Deferred Compensation Plan for Corporate Employees

Rules: Employees may contribute a percentage of their compensation or the legal maximum per year, tax-deferred. The employer may contribute the difference between the employee contribution and $30,000, also tax-deferred. The more your employer contributes, usually called "matching," the better the plan. The contribution limit will be increased for inflation over the years. The best 401(k) plans are those that offer mutual funds as investment options.

2. **403(b)—Deferred Compensation Plan (tax-sheltered annuity) for Public School and Nonprofit Organization Employees**
Rules: Employees may contribute approximately 20% of compensation up to $9,500 per year, tax-deferred. The employer has the option of contributing the difference between the employee contribution and $30,000, also tax-deferred, although few, if any, employers use this option. Most public school employees are also covered by a separate pension plan over which the employee has no control. Again, the best 403(b) plans offer mutual funds as investment options.

3. **457—Deferred Compensation Plan for State, County, and City Employees**
Rules: Employees may contribute up to $7,500 per year tax-deferred. Employers may not contribute. Most municipal employees are also covered by a separate pension plan over which the employee has no control. And again, the best 457 plans (you guessed it) are those that offer mutual funds as investment options.

4. **408(k) SEP—Simplified Employee Pension Plan for Employees of Small Companies (less than twenty-five employees)**
Rules: Employees may contribute up to 15% of compensation or the legal maximum per year, tax-deferred. SEPs, like IRAs, can be contributed to until April 15th of the year following the tax year. The employer may contribute the difference between the employee contribution and $30,000, also tax-deferred. The more your employer contributes, the better the plan. And as you already know, the best SEP plans (all together now . . .) *are those that offer mutual funds as investment options.*

I. Request a Description of Your Retirement Plan

If you don't know where you are going, you will probably end up somewhere else.
—**Laurence J. Peter**

■ SCENARIO

Matt and Jenny are excited about the benefits of their companies' retirement program options. Every so often, they receive literature and questionnaires regarding their company-sponsored plan, however, they've both been too busy to take the time to understand fully their benefits and options. They know they should maximize

their benefits, but the choices are confusing, at times, leaving them even more un-
sure about what actions they should take.

If you are fortunate enough to work for a company with a qualified plan
to help you save, use it! This is one of the best ways to save for your future.

This plan might be called a 401(k) if you work for a corporation, a
403(b) if you work for a nonprofit organization, a Keogh plan if you are self-
employed (or work for a sole proprietorship or partnership). With these types
of plans you can have money deducted straight from your paycheck before
taxes, and before you ever see it. This is the easiest and most beneficial way to
save, because not only do you get the tax advantage, but you are also forced
into saving every single payday. In most plans you can direct your investments into different types of mutual funds, according to risk and return.

In most cases, it's wisest for individuals to contribute the **maximum** to
their company-sponsored plans (usually up to 15% of earned income) before
ever opening any other type of investment account. It makes sense to invest
before taxes first, before you wander into outside investments.

The drawback to most of these plans is that you are usually penalized for
early withdrawal (before age fifty-nine and a half). In most plans, however,
you can get your money early for an emergency (subject to IRS definitions)
or as a down payment on your primary residence.

In any case, it's wise to **ask your employer for a detailed description of your plan** and find out about your eligibility to participate.

Once you get a copy of the plan's rules, requirements, and investment options, you'll want to do several things:

1. **Determine how much you can contribute.** Fiddle with your budget.
   Shift your "savings" money into this column if you won't need it immediately. If you can put up to ten or fifteen percent of your monthly
   income, before taxes, start there.

2. **Request that your retirement savings be deducted from your paycheck.** If
   available, this is a great benefit to you. Your before-tax contributions
   go into your retirement kitty before your grubby little hands get a
   chance to spend the money.

3. **Decide on appropriate investment choices.** Most plans offer a "menu" of
   mutual funds that you can invest your retirement savings into. When
   you're young, you'll want to lean more into stock and growth funds.
   Later, you'll want to shift your assets into more conservative vehicles.

If you don't have a plan at work, or aren't eligible, you can contribute to an IRA (individual retirement account). But no matter what your situation, there is a way to save some money on a tax-deductible (or before-tax) basis. For more tools and explanation, check out *Grow Rich Slowly* from Viking, *The Merrill Lynch Guide to Retirement Planning* from Underwood & Brown, or visit *www.schwab.com* on the Web. If you more need help, seek a tax or financial advisor.

To Do:

■ Request a detailed description of your company's retirement program.

II. Know Your Retirement Plan Options

Before you decide to retire, take a week off and watch daytime television.
—Anonymous

■ EXERCISE:

Most retirement plans can be broken down into three parts: **contributions, investment options, and withdrawal options.** *From the following list, find the answer to each question as you consider each part of your retirement program.*

Question	Answer
Contributions	
Do I qualify to contribute to an IRA? How much?	_____
What kind of plan does my employer offer:	
401(k), 403(b), 457, or SEP?	_____
How much can I deposit each year into all plans?	_____
How much of my contribution is deductible from my taxable income?	_____
Does my employer give me any matching funds? What percentage?	_____
Investment Options	
What are the choices for investments?	_____
How often can I change investments?	_____
Should I move my money now to a better investment?	_____
How can I earn the best returns?	_____
Withdrawal Options	
At what age can I withdraw my money with no penalty?	_____

What is the penalty if I withdraw before then? _____

Under what conditions (disability or financial hardship) can I withdraw my money with no penalty? _____

Can I borrow from my plan? How much? _____

Should I withdraw my money in a lump sum, annuity payments, or use the RA rollover rules? _____

Once you've sifted through the literature or contacted an in-house expert and answered each question completely, you'll find yourself with a pretty good handle on the workings of your company's retirement program. Then, you'll be able to maximize its benefits to help you reach your retirement goals. Otherwise, you'll wind up in a trailer park in Kansas. It's the trailer park capital of the world, though, so you get to keep your bragging rights.

Our government wants you to save for your own retirement (it costs them less), so they offer encouragement in the form of tax savings—now (tax-deductible contributions) and later (tax-deferred growth).

To Do:

■ Get a handle on the benefits and requirements of your retirement program.

■ 5. DON'T EVEN REMOTELY COUNT ON SOCIAL "SECURITY"

Nothing is easier than spending public money. It does not appear to belong to anybody. The temptation is overwhelming to bestow it on somebody.

—Calvin Coolidge

■ SCENARIO

Matt and Jenny have been paying into the Social Security system (via FICA) for some time now, even though they're not exactly pumped about it. Still, they figure, they'll be able to draw on their "savings" one day and all their retirement days will be hunky-dory.

First off, Social Security is not designed to be your personal savings plan. It's a tax. There's no accountant in D.C. managing "your" retirement money. Today, it takes nearly all of your contributory tax to fund the payments to existing retirees, who paid their tax in their working years. One problem with the system is that we're all living longer and these assets don't go as far as they used to. (What a friggin' surprise!) The other major problem with the system is that it gives very little consideration to "how much" you actually contributed. You can bet your private tattoo location that your grandpa put in about one-tenth of what he's drawing down now. (Remember, he used to work for a dollar a day, right? Let's see, seven percent of one dollar . . .)

But, to be fair, it's not their fault. Our government told them that if they bit the bullet and paid this tax, they'd "be taken care of in old age." So, our parents and grandparents did their duty and paid the "security" tax. Now they're pissed at the thought of a reduction in benefits (the AARP fights like hell to make sure they get their due), and I don't blame them.

But it's a sucker tax—for the government *and* the taxpayers. It makes absolutely no economic sense to offer an *unlimited* benefit in trade for a *defined* contribution. Who would buy a car without a price tag? (Let's see . . . a new Corolla? That'll be a monthly payment of whatever we decide for the rest of your life. Duh, that's fair. I'll take it. Just gimme the car.) That's effectively the route we chose with Social Security. (Send you monthly checks for life? Sure, sure, sure. Just gimme the dough.) Our government officials made a stupid bet: they traded short-term tax income for their promise to support us forever—which they can't do. Unless Florida secedes . . .

Oh, and here's the kicker: IT'S THE LAW. You can't get around paying it, even though you know darned well that they're pillaging our hard-earned money with all the care a desert cactus receives from a bulldozer.

In defense, the Social Security system does limit the amount you have to pay once you've reached a certain point for the year. ('Course next year, the tally starts all over again.) Still, it is very naive to think that this is an "equitable" sharing tax arrangement. If you live long enough, you'll "win" by taking out more than you ever contributed. If you die, you lose anyway—which, dear heart, is what they're betting on.

Social Security benefits might be one source of income when you retire, but the bulk of your retirement income will come from other sources. The figures below represent the maximum amount you can expect to receive from Social Security annually if you retire at age sixty-five in the years indicated.

Maximum annual benefits of Social Security *
1990. . . . . $10,747
1995. . . . . $11,384
2000. . . . . $12,663

* Source: Shearson Lehman Brothers

The greatest single source of income for retired people today is personal savings. Most of your retirement income is likely to depend on *you*, not on Uncle Sam. I'm sorry, but that's life as we know it.

The income you'll receive from your Social Security benefits is based on how much you have earned, how long you have worked, and when you retire. You can **call the Social Security Administration (1-800-772-1213; ask for form SSA-7004)** to get an estimate of the benefits you would receive based upon your projected retirement date. You'll feel like an insignificant little bug when you get their automated answering computer menu, but hang in there. Once you get your report, you can begin making plans based on the retirement income figures they give you.

6. START YOUR OWN PERSONAL RETIREMENT PLAN

Live your life each day as you would climb a mountain. An occasional glance toward the summit keeps the goal in mind, but many beautiful scenes are to be observed from each new vantage point. Climb slowly, steadily, enjoying each passing moment; and the view from the summit will serve as a fitting climax for the journey.

—Harold V. Melchert

■ SCENARIO

Matt and Jenny have been hearing (every year around tax time) about the benefits of an individual retirement account (IRA). They're in good enough shape to participate now and they want to take advantage of all the money-saving strategies they can.

For the most part, a personal retirement plan in America is an individual retirement account.

An IRA is an account you set up specifically for your retirement savings and investments. In an IRA, your investment compounds tax-deferred until you take it out. If you qualify, your contributions to the plan may also be tax-deductible. If you have an employer-sponsored retirement plan, you may not qualify for a tax deduction; however, your money still grows on a tax-deferred basis until you take it out.

Here's the point: if you aren't contributing to a company-sponsored retirement plan, open an IRA. If you have a company-sponsored retirement plan, you may still qualify for a partial deduction (I recommend that you see an accountant or financial advisor). Either way, deductible or not, your account grows tax-deferred. No taxes on gains and interest are due until you withdraw the money at retirement.

Let's say you contribute just $2,000 per year to your IRA for the next thirty years—your total out of pocket would be $60,000, right? Assuming a 12% annual return, your retirement account would be worth $483,000 at the end of that period. On the other hand, the same $2,000 annual savings outside an IRA would net you only about $273,000, since you've been paying taxes along the way. That's a huge difference for just using the benefits you're offered, huh? And remember: Your IRA contribution is completely "tax-deductible"—a savings you've gained along the way that our little example doesn't even consider. Not bad, right?

One other mistake that people make is not getting started soon enough—they'll "make it up later," they believe. Big no-no. Here's why:

Let's say you start contributing $2,000 yearly to your IRA at age twenty-one, which you continue only until age thirty, then you stop. You've put in $20,000 and won't shell out another IRA nickel, but you just let it grow at a rate of 8%. At age fifty, you have an IRA balance of $145,841.

On the other hand, let's say that you don't do a damn thing until age thirty, but then, as you've vowed, you stick away $2,000 every single year until age fifty—total out of pocket is double, $40,000. At age fifty, your account balance is $98,846. Still not bad, but in the first scenario, you've made almost fifty thousand dollars more and invested twenty thousand dollars less—all thanks to the power of compound interest.

Make sure you understand the laws before you open an account. There are catches; for example, if you withdraw the money before age fifty-nine and a half, you would incur a 10% penalty in addition to the taxes. However, you can avoid the penalty by withdrawing your money in essentially equal payments (based on mortality tables, you "even out" your distributions over the course of your remaining life expectancy—neat loophole if you really need the money to live on).

If you have questions, most brokerage firms, banks, or accounting firms have brochures that explain the rules. Next, we'll discuss the rules in more detail, but make sure you get professional advice before you dive in. The rules change often, and you'll need to keep abreast.

Moral of the story: start early, start now! You've got the time to let investment compounding work its magic, so use it. Thank you.

Look how far you've come. The future's so bright, you've got to wear shades.

To Do:

- Consider opening and contributing annually to an IRA.
- Invest in a pair of sunglasses.

Any intelligent fool can make things bigger, more complex. It takes a touch of genius—and a lot of courage—to move in the opposite direction.
—**E. F. Schumacher, British economist**

■ **SCENARIO**

Matt and Jenny are making it a habit to sock away as much moola as they can into their IRAs. They're planning to be richer than her grandma's coffee cake by the time they retire. Which means that they've got to get started right away, get IRA savvy, and make smart investment choices.

Here are some IRA Do's and Don'ts—tips I've picked up that'll make your IRA sing like a birdy:

DO make smart IRA investments. Many people make the mistake of confusing the IRA tax-structure with the investments *inside the IRA;* the two require separate consideration. An IRA *is not an investment.* It is merely an account than can hold investments. Even though banks sometimes post their so-called "IRA rates" in their store windows, what they're really posting is their CD or money market rates that you *may choose* as an investment option *inside* your IRA. Your IRA money can be invested in many types of investments, including: CDs, stocks, bonds, and mutual funds.

DO exercise your IRA rollover options. If you're changing jobs or retiring, the IRS rules allow you to "rollover" your entire company retirement plan—401(k), 403(b), 457, or SEP—to an IRA without paying taxes. Make sure you really do "rollover" your retirement account, though, by having your employer transfer the money directly into your IRA. If you actually "take possession" of the money—even if it's only to walk the check to the bank—you'll get hit with a 20% withholding requirement that'll be sent to the IRS for potential taxes. You'll get the money back if you do "rollover" your plan into an IRA, but you just gotta know that getting money *from* the IRS is going to be a hassle.

DON'T be *too* conservative with your IRA investments. Since your IRA is effectively money set aside for retirement— which is presumably a long time away—you'll want to invest in vehicles (such as stock mutual funds) that make the best use of this "time." If you have ten years, or more, until retirement, you have plenty of time to benefit from any market cycles and down-turns and still wind up better than if you'd taken a more conservative approach. Remember, the IRA's growth and interest accumulate on a "tax-deferred" basis, so you'll really want to give higher performance your best shot.

DON'T invest your IRA in a tax shelter. An IRA is already tax-sheltered by nature. You cannot take the deduction twice, so avoid tax-sheltered investments, which are usually more restrictive.

DON'T neglect your IRA "portfolio." Just because you've "set-aside" this money and don't intend to "touch it," don't be negligent about monitoring and managing your IRA account's performance. It's still an investment account, sometimes a substantial one, and you want to keep on top of it routinely. If it starts to stink up the joint, consider making some changes.

Your IRA will, over time, most likely become your most significant source of retirement funding. If you do your homework regarding the complete rules and stay on top of your investment choices, you'll find a big fat account awaiting you on retirement day.

The law's made to take care o' rascals.

—George Eliot

■ SCENARIO

Matt and Jenny are sobbing piteously, having sifted through pages and pages of IRA rules, requirements, and exceptions. They've found that there are rules for contribution, rules for investment, rules for distributions—and exceptions to just about everything. They've heard about "traditional," "Roth," and "educational" IRAs, and they're totally discombobulated. They thought IRAs were supposed to help them retire rich, not kill them early.

Here's the gig: the IRA, while an excellent idea for investors, has become a broad target for congressional tinkering. Hardly anyone of influence can resist adding their two cents' worth of "betterment" as a gift to the people. Consequently, the rules, which were once very simple, now require professional (and costly) counsel in order to fully understand (and exploit) them.

There are basically two IRA benefits that need to be distinguished from one another:

1. **Tax-deductible.** Contributions made to your IRA may be deductible from current income.

2. **Tax-deferred.** Growth of your investments and interest accumulation within your IRA account is allowed to do so on a tax-deferred basis; you don't pay taxes until you actually withdraw monies from the ac-

count. (Usually, this means you'll pay less tax overall because, at retirement, most people are in lower tax brackets.)

There are also two ways the IRS gets their money:

1. Penalties. Early withdrawals before the age of fifty-nine and a half, barring any of the exceptions below, are subject to a 10% penalty on the amount of the distribution.

2. Taxes. You will also pay taxes on any distribution you take, before or after the age of fifty-nine and a half. This is only fair, really, since you contributed the money on a "before-tax" basis in the first place.

Here are the basic contribution and distribution "rules" regarding IRAs:

1. Contributions. You can open an account and/or make deposits into your IRA up until April 15th of the following year you earned the qualifying income. *If you participate in a company-sponsored retirement plan,* you're legally allowed to **deduct** your total contribution, up to a maximum of: $2,000 for yourself and $2,000 for your spouse—as long as you're not declaring less **income** than your contribution, and as long as (starting in 1998) you don't make more than $30–40,000 (single filers) and $50–60,000 (joint filers). *Provided neither spouse contributes to an employer-related retirement plan,* you may contribute the deductible maximum ($2,000) to an IRA, regardless of total income.

2. Distributions. You may withdraw money from your IRA any time you wish. However, if you are under fifty-nine and a half and withdraw any part of your money, you must pay the 10% penalty on the amount withdrawn. All withdrawals of tax-deferred money are added to your taxable income for the year. You may also begin withdrawing from your IRA in periodic payments, using the life-expectancy payout rules, any time you wish, penalty free. [If you need the money to live on, the law allows you to "even out" your distributions over your remaining "expected" life without penalty, as long as you stick to the schedule. (E.g., say you're sixty years old with a "life expectancy" of eighty—from the table, you can't guess on your own—and you have $100,000 in your IRA. Well, that'll be a rough distribution of $5,000 per year for the next twenty years. Of course, you must also calculate an expected rate into your schedule.) But don't try it without consulting a good accountant first.]

Big changes were made in 1996, and more are expected. Here's my best guess on the major changes in the IRA rules:

Penalty-free withdrawals for first-time home buyers. You and your spouse can each withdraw up to $10,000, without penalty, in order to buy your first home. But you still have to pay the taxes due on the distribution.

Penalty-free withdrawals for educational expense. You may withdraw monies from your IRA, without penalties, in order to pay for education expenses for your children or grandchildren.

Non-deductible "educational" IRAs for your children. You can set aside up to $500 per year for your child's benefit. You can't deduct the contribution, but the earnings are tax-deferred, and the distributions are tax-free if used for educational expenses such as tuition, room and board, books, and supplies and equipment.

Penalty-free withdrawals for medical expense. You don't have to pay penalties (usually 10%) on monies you withdraw for the purpose of paying medical expenses—as long as you're under fifty-nine and a half and the expenses don't exceed 7.5% of your adjusted gross income. You still have to pay the taxes due on the monies you withdraw.

Penalty-free withdrawals for health insurance for those on unemployment. If you receive unemployment compensation (under federal or state law) for at least twelve weeks, you can withdraw "penalty-free" monies, although you have to pay the taxes, in order to pay your medical insurance.

NEW "non-deductible" Roth IRA is all the rage. You can make "non-deductible" contributions to what is coming to be called a "Roth" IRA. The major benefit is that you can also withdraw your monies without penalty or taxes, as long as you leave the money in the IRA for at least five years. You may convert "traditional" IRAs to "Roth" IRAs without penalty, under certain conditions, but you may still owe the taxes due on the distribution. The contribution limits are still $2,000 annually—for Roth and traditional IRA combined.

Roth IRAs are to operate under the rules that apply to regular IRAs, we think, but here's my best summary of how a "Roth" IRA stacks up against a "Traditional" IRA:

	Traditional IRA	Roth IRA
Annual dollar limit	$2,000	$2,000
Percentage of compensation limit	100%	100%
Contribution allowed after age 70½	NO	YES
Distributions must start by age 70½	YES	NO
Accepts tax-free rollovers from IRAs	YES	NO
Accepts taxable rollovers from regular IRAs	NO	YES
Accepts tax-free rollovers from Roth IRAs	NO	YES
Accepts rollovers from employer plans	YES	NO
Contributions might be deductible	YES	NO
Distributions might be tax-free	NO	YES
Basis recovery approach	Prorata	FIFO
AGI limit on allowable contributions	N/A	$115,000 (Single)/ $160,000 (Joint) AGI
Limit on Rollovers from Regular IRAs	N/A	$100,000

Overall, the IRA is a great deal; it offers tremendous benefits for your retirement savings (the key word being "retirement"—accessing your money early is where you get hit) because it encourages you to save and invest for the long term by making your contributions **tax-deductible** and the earnings **tax-deferred.** You still pay taxes on the distributions, but, once retired, you may find that your tax bracket has lowered, saving you money overall. Remember, the biggest benefit is really the compounding power of your IRA investments; avoiding that annual tax bite allows more of your money to remain at work.

Suburbia:
Looking Toward Responsible Retirement, Insurance, and College Planning

Matt and Jenny, shackled by the PTA and a budding clarinetist prodigy, plot their distant escape from suburbia.

First, have a definite, clear, practical ideal—a goal, an objective. Second, have the necessary means to achieve your ends—wisdom, money, materials and methods. Third, adjust all your means to that end.

—Aristotle

■ 1. ACHIEVE LIFE'S FIVE MAJOR FINANCIAL GOALS

This is life—and it is passing. What are we waiting for?

—Richard L. Evans

■ SCENARIO

Matt and Jenny are starting to make great financial progress. Their debt is under control, and they're now beginning to think maturely about the future. Rather than being content to just live month to month, or even year to year, Matt and Jenny are working toward achieving their major life financial goals. But that is a daunting prospect. Which should they tackle now, and which later? Their tendency has been to put off the difficult actions until a better time rolls around, but they've been at this long enough now to know there is no better time. They agree that the sooner they can prioritize their financial goals and dreams, the sooner they'll achieve them.

Most of us have several major life financial goals that benchmark our arrival at certain levels. Like our first car or first apartment these new thresholds serve as the summits that hold our attention during the ascent; they also serve as "points of no return" as our lives are forever altered by having passed over them.

For the most part, we all share **five major life financial goals;** each not only represents a certain stage of accomplishment but also serves as a major emotional bookmark in our life's story—a ceremonial announcement of our financial growth and maturity, if you will. No doubt, you'll achieve many other successes along the way, but the most triumphant milestones of your financial life will probably occur on the day you:

   I.   **Burn Your Mortgage**
  II.   **Watch Your Children Graduate**
 III.   **Become a Millionaire**
  IV.   **Do What You Came to Do**
   V.   **Leave a Legacy**

Also notice that each is stated in terms of an *emotionally rich* day or event. This is an important distinction to make because we all tend to gravitate toward emotionally compelling situations. We want to *feel* good, remember? Even though the monthly savings required to send your children to college may seem uncomfortable in the moment, the image of them proudly crossing the stage warms you up to see the more important perspective. Make sense?

So, an important part of goal setting has to do with making an *emotional connection* to the feelings you'll experience by achieving that goal. And the best way to make that emotional connection is by asking yourself *questions* that will offer detailed, emotionally charged answers that are compelling enough to gravitate toward. For example, when you think of each of your **five major life financial goals,** you may want to consider the following questions:

  I) The day you **burn your mortgage.** *What will it feel like when you and your family set fire to that long-standing mortgage debt? When you look around your home—that you own completely—does it look (and feel) a bit different? How does that make you feel?*

 II) The day you **watch your children graduate** from college. *How proud does it make you feel to know that you've supported your children in their endeavors? Was it worth the planning and effort to know that you've helped them make a positive entrance into the "real" world?*

III) The day you **become a millionaire.** *What happens when your accountant calls and informs you that you've passed the magic number? What sort of pride, confidence, and power comes with the experience of becoming a millionaire?*

 IV) The day you finally have time to **do what you came to do.** *How does it feel to finally retire and get on with the next phase of your life's goals? What does it feel like to plot a financially unencumbered journey around the world? What dreams are you now free to resume?*

  V) When you're finally able to **leave a legacy**. *What's important about knowing that "you're all right now," that you've taken care of your own needs and can now afford to leave a legacy for your family and friends? What kind of difference did you make so far in the world? What kind of difference can you make going forward, now that your financial needs are met completely?*

Getting comfortable attaching these kinds of "future memories" to your dreams will give them tremendous power; they'll seem to come to life, stirring you to act on behalf of their realization.

In the coming pages, we'll discuss each financial goal, or "milestone," in detail. But, for now, the most powerful action you can take toward their actualization is to simply PLAN TO ACHIEVE THEM by making an *emotional investment* in them. It's not that hard to set unfeeling numbers goals, but once you have a flavor for what it *feels* like to achieve them, it's very hard to turn your back on them for very long; these pleasant experiences will always be calling you toward them. Then set some *concrete* short-term and long-term goals that will help you work your way toward these special days of achievement.

Finally, make it a point to memorize these **five major life financial goals** and the feelings associated with each's success. Add to the list if there's another that's been left out. Remember, these things don't just happen. They require commitment and discipline and action.

■ EXERCISE: FACE YOUR TIME HORIZON

As we move through life, our priorities tend to shift. As we enter new phases, usually marked by ten-year periods, we typically "let go" of old desires—whether we've achieved them, or not—and look forward to new ones. So, I believe it's best to anticipate these changes in our financial status in advance. That way, we can focus our energies into the areas that are most important to us **now,** *pushing for their success, and then comfortably slide into the next phase.*

Following, we'll use our five major life financial goals as an example. Please note, however, that the period of focus is not the same as the period of achievement. We tend to focus on things we haven't learned yet. Once they've become master skills—while they may still remain a big part of our life—we tend to move on to focus on other areas.

If we miss our window of focus, we lose a tremendous amount of the value inherent in the process; you can't plan for a day that's already here.

We all tend to have passionate concerns about similar financial issues, which change over time. The best way to achieve the results we want is to maximize those desires by striking when our concern and energy are already "focused" on those areas. Then, by anticipating our next phase of "focus" beforehand, we can move forward, while leaving no goal or desire unfinished.

There is an age range, a "focus" period, when we're the most interested in achieving our major goals:

Major Goals	Age & Planning/Focus Period
I. **BURN YOUR MORTGAGE**	25–35
This plan begins when you take out your first mortgage.	
II. **WATCH YOUR CHILDREN GRADUATE**	40–50
Plan early in order to save enough. School's not cheap.	
III. **BECOME A MILLIONAIRE**	45–55
You should be starting to build major equity by this point.	
IV. **DO WHAT YOU CAME TO DO**	55–65
At retirement, you begin to plan for the "second" half of life.	
V. **LEAVE A LEGACY**	65+
Once you've climbed the mountain, you'll want to help others as well.	

Don't worry. You don't have to get your datebook out yet. I just want you to start thinking in terms of the long term. A little focus now can save a lot of heartache later.

You don't want to wait until your kid's applying at Harvard to start making financial arrangements. By the same token, once you're retired, it's too late to plan; you're there! Once you've signed the mortgage, you're done. You don't shop afterward. If you do plan ahead of time, however, you should have no trouble in reaching these five major life financial goals.

Here's the exercise:

Let's assume you're going to live to be a hundred years old. First, on the calendar below, **mark your age;** make sure you mark out all the years that have come and gone. Then, find an age at which you'll wish to have achieved each of the five financial life goals and write it underneath. Here's an example:

1	11	21	31	41	51	61	71	81	91
X	X	X							
2	12	22	32	42	52	62	72	82	92
X	X	X				**RETIREE**			
3	13	23	33	43	53	63	73	83	93
X	X	X			**$1MM**				
4	14	24	34	44	54	64	74	84	94
X	X	X							
5	15	25	35	45	55	65	75	85	95
X	X	X	**MTGE**						
6	16	26	36	46	56	66	76	86	96
X	X	X		**EDUC**					
7	17	27	37	47	57	67	77	87	97
X	X	X							
8	18	28	38	48	58	68	78	88	98
X	X	X					**LEGCY**		
9	19	29	39	49	59	69	79	89	99
X	X	X							
10	20	**AGE** 30	40	50	60	70	80	90	100
X	X	**NOW**							

For one thing, I hope taking a look at your life's calendar serves as a sort of "wake-up call." We don't really have that much time TO DO, HAVE, BE, and ACHIEVE all we're capable of—and the past is gone. Part of getting *A Kick in the Assets* is the realization that life is short and priorities must be handled NOW.

I. Life Goal Focus: Burn Your Mortgage

Before everything else, getting ready is the secret of success.

—**Henry Ford, Sr.**

■ SCENARIO

Matt and Jenny have signed for a thirty-year mortgage in order to buy their dream home. Even though it seems like an eternity away, they've already been thinking about the day they'll own their home outright, lock, stock, and barrel. But then reality sets in. They know they'll be buying other homes in the future; probably making thirty-year commitments for them as well. Do they really have to occupy a home for thirty years in order to pay it off completely?

The best way to ensure that you eventually burn your mortgage is by **picking the date beforehand,** when you buy your home, then never paying on a home beyond that point—even though you'll most likely be taking out several mortgages throughout your life.

For example: let's say you commit to a thirty-year mortgage in the year 2000, which would be due to be burned in 2030. Right? Well, in a few years, you'll probably sell that home and take out another thirty-year mortgage, then another, then another, and so on. But each time you sign a new mortgage, your burning date gets pushed back a few years. A good way to ensure that you eventually reach your goal is to consistently make payments adequate enough to pay your home down by 2030. Even if you take out another thirty-year mortgage later (that now goes well past your initial burn date), you can make extra principal payments that will pay off the loan early, by the original year, 2030. Got it?

Otherwise you'll be paying on a mortgage until the reaper moves in, and dodging your mortgage lender is not a good way to spend your golden years.

II. Life Goal Focus: Watch Your Children Graduate

Success depends on previous preparation, and without such preparation there is sure to be failure.

—Confucius

■ SCENARIO

Matt and Jenny want to get a jump on college costs for their future children. They want their family to have the best opportunities in life and feel responsible for assisting as best they can. They also know how expensive college can be, and, in looking ahead, they feel they should start saving right away. They're willing to make some sacrifices but know how important it is to let their investments work hard as well.

Good news: Given America's resources and respect for education, it's likely that your child could receive the best education of any student in history.

Bad news: History's best education commands history's highest prices.

In twenty years, the annual cost of your child's college will be around

forty thousand big ones; that's for a four-year public university. A four-year private school will be **twice** that amount, which gives us a good rule of thumb (2X) when comparing *public versus private* education. All things considered, a public education is a really good deal since college students bear such a small amount of the total costs themselves. Twenty years from now, in order to shell out ONE HUNDRED SIXTY GRAND (forty thou a year) for tuition, room and board, books, and other fees, you'll need to be saving about $240 per month at a 9% investment return ($480 per month for the private schools). Even though you've slaved for years, you'll at least be able to take pride in the opportunity you've provided: little Johnny will get to sleep next to a keg of Heineken for four years, while you're mowing lawns on the weekends. Obviously, if you can swing a higher return, get your kid to take a job, win the lottery, or take out student loans, you can get by with less savings (and mowing). But remember, the longer your money has to compound, the less strain will be put upon you at college time.

Here are some suggestions for giving your child a shot at the dream education.

1. **Decide which type of university or college your child will attend: public or private?**

2. **Call the nearest University and get their estimated annual costs,** then **double it once for every ten years** until your child arrives on campus. I've done the homework on college costs, so trust me: they've doubled every ten years for the past thirty years. Besides tuition, don't forget room and board, and other expenses such as rock concerts, parking tickets, and bail bonds. Then sit back and enjoy the fruits of your labor.

3. **Work backward** from your annual cost figure to come up with a **monthly savings amount.** Don't forget to factor in a return of between 7% and 11% percent (about what a decent stock fund will give). Then start sticking it away. Don't wait until your movie deal hits. Do it now. The interest accumulation will be a huge factor if you start early.

III. Life Goal Focus: Become a Millionaire

The populace may hiss me, but when I go home and think of my money I applaud myself.
—Horace

■ **SCENARIO**

Matt and Jenny have decided to shoot for the brass ring: **millionaire status.** *They know it's a lofty goal, but they feel that with time, hard work, and a bit of money smarts, they can do it.*

A million bucks doesn't go as far as it used to; in Texas oil-baron circles, a *hundred million* dollars is referred to as a "unit"—you know, like the first building block. Still, a million-dollar net worth is a damn good start. Even with the erosion of inflation, you can live pretty well with that kind of bread. Plus, having a substantial net worth lends itself to all kinds of opportunities that "being broke" doesn't consider. As of 1997, there were an estimated *one million* millionaires in America. So, this whole idea of being a millionaire is becoming somewhat commonplace, which is great. There's enough opportunity here, and I've seen many, many very average people achieve this goal. It's certainly doable.

The reason I bring it up is that I want you to get used to being around that word: "millionaire." Say it a few times into the mirror, let it roll around your tongue like Thurston Howell III would. Begin to see yourself as someone capable of being worth a million bucks and more. You are. You have more than enough potential.

It'll take time and discipline, but you can get there if you use the time wisely. You've already begun to save at least ten percent of every dollar you earn. Invest it wisely and, given time, you'll make it.

Here's the reality, though, and a point I'm adamant about: very few people ever "piggyback" their way to tremendous wealth. Investing offers excellent returns considering the effort you really put in; you're really just lending your money to people (or organizations) who can use your dough more effectively than you can. Right?

I mean, buying shares in, say, Microsoft or Coca-Cola basically states that you *really* think that the money is better used in their hands. And, for the most part, it probably is. They've exhibited a knack for making investors, and themselves, considerable profits. But I'd just like you to consider why that is so: *why are all the good opportunities for your capital somewhere else? In someone else's care?*

Here's a quick thought in answer: the most wealthy people in our society are the small to medium business owners, hands down. These are people who have learned to *create* value with their sweat, brains, *and* capital—the key word here being "create."

Allow me to rail on this "create" concept for a moment with an example. Let's form a simple economy, OK? In this simple economy we have *only* two apples—a *Fuji* apple and a *Granny Smith*—which we trade back and forth, back and forth, back and forth, whenever we decide we'd rather have one over the other. (OK, so this is a crude, unbelievable barter system, but you get my point; it could be beads we're trading for food, or computers we sell in order to pay the rent. Still, the idea I'm trying to relate is that we're a bunch of Ferengi who trade things we don't want for things we do.) Now, given that we're good at this type of barter, we've gotten very sophisticated: we now use efficient delivery systems to cart these apples back and forth overnight; then we hire "apple brokers" to convince the other party to swap again; then we discover the "velocity of money" in that we can trade quickly and keep ourselves occupied; **finally we discover the "commission" whereby we can take a "bite" out of each apple as it transacts.**

OK, so everybody in this little apple economy is pretty happy. They're busy, can eat apples until their eyes pop out, and can get exactly *which* apple they desire.

But one day . . . a man walks into the picture holding a giant, succulent *Jonathan* apple. (Gasp of awe.) The apple-jockeys are amazed: their economy has increased by half again because this guy created a new commodity. They trade it back and forth, taking bigger bites now, getting richer with every pass of the hands.

Until the next day . . . the same man walks in with a giant bushel of *Jonathan* apples. (Teary-eyed sigh of human amazement.) The apple-traders freak out; their economy has expanded to immense proportions. So they take bigger bites as they trade back and forth at lightning speed.

Until the next day . . . the man arrives with two thousand donkey carts filled to the gullet with *Jonathan* apples. Holy shit! Again, they delight in their good fortune by trading and eating to lusty proportions.

So, now the man hires the apple-traders to build him a magnificent home and a vast apple orchard. (Being the little Ferengis that they are, they take the gig in order to swipe a few apples from the job.)

If you were expecting a happy ending, don't. **This is a tragedy:** these little peons never clue in to the idea that they could **grow their own apples**—they could create their own fortunes and quit squabbling and haggling over apples for survival. If they'd just learned to create, they wouldn't have died of the apple-induced dysentery that swept the village; they, too, could have built magnificent homes and vast apple orchards.

I tell that story—and I sincerely hope you get it—to explain one concept that I see keeps many people from ever achieving the lifestyle they deserve: *in our society, you can either be a **middler,** transacting in the realities of shuffling money and resources around (in the middle of every deal, with your finger in the pie)—or you can be a **creator,** creating products, services, opportunities, and jobs that **expand our economy** to everyone's benefit.*

So, I invite you to take a look around. Are the wealthy people you admire **creators** or **middlers?** And then take a good look at how you spend your days. *Are you constantly looking for ways to create? Or are you chasing the apples in transaction?*

I've done both at different points in my life, and I can tell you in no uncertain terms: **if you possess the understanding and ability to create wealth, you will have more than enough in this lifetime.**

A strong statement, I know, but pay attention to what's happening in our society and decide for yourself if that makes sense. Check out the Forbes 100 richest people in America and see if you can find one that didn't *create* as a way of life. See if you can find even one middler in the mix. See if you can discover one that didn't create a new form of distribution (Sam Walton), a more effective way to ship (FedEx), the perfect burger (Wendy's), the biggest blockbuster of all time (*E.T.* or *Star Wars,* depending on your camp), or a technology movement that changed the world (Microsoft)—**all out of nothing but vision and dedication.** Look around. Our free-enterprise system rewards *creators* in staggering proportions, while the rest hustle around for old apples.

IV. Life Goal Focus: Do What You Came to Do

The thing I should wish to obtain with money would be leisure with security.
—Bertrand Russell

■ SCENARIO

Matt and Jenny have so many plans for their future. They want to travel the world and own the finest of everything. They'd love to sail the seven seas, dine at the White House, and coauthor a book about their journeys. They know that, with their busy schedules and commitments these days, most of these goals and plans will have to wait for later in their lives. Still, if they plan right and work hard, they will have the time and money to fulfill their fondest desires.

Retirement is the practical time for many people to give life to their most exotic wishes. Don't get me wrong, we can all achieve dreams during our working years, it's just that the amount of time and finances required for "big" dreams are often only available to people after they retire. And there's a horrible catch-22. Nearly 75 million Americans aren't saving enough for retirement, let alone the kind of retirement of which big dreams are made, which means they'll most likely be working longer. They'll probably be leaving a good deal of their dreams on the table for the sake of earning a living. Still, a rewarding retirement is something we can all aspire to. If we plan and take action, we can build a significant nest egg that will, someday, support our dreams.

Here's the point: if you're putting in your time at work, plugging away, thinking only about retirement, you must consider the idea that you may not be in the most rewarding or inspiring situation. **If you can't or won't change that situation and chase down your dreams now, it's imperative that you sock away plenty of money for retirement.** Sit down with a financial planner and plot an achievable course. If you don't, you run the risk of becoming like so many people in our workforce: lifeless, jaded, and burned-out. If retirement dreams are what's keeping you going, you absolutely must do everything you can to keep that fire alive.

Our dreams are intimately tied to our sense of purpose. Below you'll find an exercise that will set you on course to identifying and refining your larger life mission to help you separate the dreams of today from those you can pack away for your future retirement.

■ EXERCISE: CONSIDER YOUR LARGER LIFEWORK PATH

As we contemplate our financial future, recalling our sense of purpose gives us the kind of clarity that drives success. To be everything we are capable of being, and see the financial results we deserve, **we must discover our lifework.**

DEFINITION: *Lifework*—A person's life mission, characterized by vision and purpose.

Here is my lifework statement. My Lifework is to help people reach their financial dreams and elevate the quality of their lives.

Please notice that my lifework definition is not measured in terms of numbers, or income, but rather in service—**a driving vision I've committed myself to regardless of the outcome.**

Earlier, when we talked about **purpose,** we focused mainly on ourselves—what we wanted to stand for and what we wanted our lives to be about. In order to achieve huge financial success in the world of business, however, we must focus on and fill the needs of **others.** In order for other people to see value in our product or service, it must meet their needs. This is why developing a lifework statement defines the benefits **other** people will derive from our efforts. **It's a declaration of service to other people.**

Before you get busy with the exercise, defining your *personal lifework statement*, let me give you some guidelines:

1. Begin with, **"My Lifework** (my mission of vision, purpose, and opportunity) **is to . . ."**
2. Focus on the need(s) and/or value(s) of **other people** (health, success, service, etc.)
3. Include **action** that defines broadly how you'll serve others (i.e., "to help others . . .").
4. Give it **congruence** with your highest values so you'll effortlessly walk your talk.

Remember, the super-successful people in your industry or profession all probably have only one common characteristic that separates them from the crowd: **a confident acceptance that the accolades they receive are in direct proportion to the high level of service they provide and value they add.** So, in your notebook, define your own *lifework*—your own personal, inspiring **mission of vision, purpose, and opportunity.**

Retirement's a good time, but NOW is a better time to **do what you came to do.**

To Do:

■ Define your lifework and live it NOW.

V. Life Goal Focus: Leave a Legacy

If you have no money, be polite.

—Danish Proverb

■ SCENARIO

Matt and Jenny would like to build a significant estate. Someday, they know, they'd like to be wealthy enough to contribute to worthwhile causes and even leave a legacy for their children. Today, however, that dream seems a million miles away. With the bills and living expenses, and limited time, they don't really see how they can get to where they want to go. They feel they should be "set" financially first, then they can afford to give.

I've interviewed and worked with many, many wealthy people and have had a hard time getting their thoughts on "giving" and "leaving a legacy" through my thick head; this one took me years to learn. Lately, however, I've been practicing their suggestions and have yielded huge rewards.

Here's the deal: learning to give and contribute is a skill separate from finances; it's a feeling of abundance that truly wealthy people possess. Now I first thought that wealthy people gave only because they could afford to—so easy for them to say and do. I've made my share of mistakes.

Let me summarize the lessons I've learned on this issue in one statement: **We all have enough. We don't have to rise above lack because we've started above it.**

As airy as that sounds, I don't know of any other way to say it. That's what I've discovered. However, we can all find ways to feel like we don't have enough. We can focus on what we don't have and how much others have. We can focus on where we want to go, instead of appreciating the great place we already are. We can focus on our lack instead of our abundance.

So, to take baby steps, it is absolutely imperative that you create a new mind-set if you're being held back by feelings of lack. **Start by learning to give and contribute in ways that don't require money.** Jot down some thoughts on this in your notebook, then get busy. You have more *time* than some, don't you? You have more *compassion* than some, don't you? You have more *ability* than some, don't you?

In order to leave a legacy, you have to give of yourself. And before money—always—you have to give some of your heart. Without that, the money isn't yours to give anyway. If you lack the desire to improve the world around you by leaving a legacy, you'll never be able to "get" enough; there's always a bigger home or more exciting conquests to pursue.

Now, for the most important legacy of all: your children. Don't make the same mistake your parents most likely made with you. Teach your children about money. It's not bad, it's not dirty, and it won't corrupt them at a young age. In fact, it may be one of the most important lessons they'll ever learn.

So, just begin to think in terms of leaving a legacy. Continually ask yourself, "How does my action and effort benefit other people? Or who could I help that's less fortunate? Who would perceive my level of 'abundance' as plenty?"

■ 2. PROTECT YOUR NEST

Men are not against you; they are merely for themselves.
          —Jan Christian Smuts, South African soldier and politician

■ SCENARIO

Matt and Jenny have been considering buying life insurance. It's an eerie thought, but one they know they must consider at some point. Their main concern, however, is not whether or not to buy life insurance—they want to; their uncertainties arise when they consider all the variables of the decision: do they buy "term" insurance or "whole life"? How much do they really need? And how do they save money, while getting the secure coverage they desire?

Buying life insurance is a major decision; which route you choose will be determined by your basic philosophy of insurance and insurance companies in general. My personal view is that insurance should be purchased in order to protect assets (such as a car or income-producer), not as an asset itself—there are better ways to invest than accumulating value (overpaid premiums) in an insurance policy. First, I'll offer some very broad definitions:

TERM LIFE—A no-frills policy that protects you only for a certain *term* (say, twenty or thirty years). This is the cheapest form of insurance because you're taking the risk of outliving your coverage. The idea here is that, in your later years, you'll hopefully have accumulated significant assets to pass to your heirs, thereby becoming *self-insured*. Term life is betting ON yourself to succeed financially.

WHOLE LIFE—A fancy policy that protects you for your *whole life*. This is the most expensive form of insurance because the insurance company is taking the risk that you'll outlive their projected life expectancy (they calculate their profits and expenses based on an average mortality table). And believe me, you pay for that peace of mind. The idea here is that you'll really need to be covered in later years, due to lack of a significant estate or assets. In a sense, whole life is betting AGAINST your succeeding financially.

Below are some basic pointers on buying life insurance.

Buy enough life insurance to cover your combined incomes.

If one spouse has a much higher income than the other, your lifestyle is probably far greater than the lower-paid spouse could afford alone. Your strategy should be to carry enough life insurance on the higher-paid spouse so that if invested at a 10% return, the income would allow the other spouse to maintain the same lifestyle. For example, a couple earning $100,000 needs **one million dollars** in death benefit coverage, but that's for term insurance, which is cheaper, not whole life.

Insure the income-producing spouse.

Approximately 30% of all the life insurance in force today is on the lives of single people who have no family responsibilities. Remember the purpose of life insurance. It should be used only to prevent a financial hardship that would be created if the insured person died. Since the chances of living through the years you are single, usually your twenties, are 985 out of 1,000, then even a small burial policy (the salesperson's last sales pitch) is not the wisest use of your money.

Replace life insurance with income sources as you grow older.

As you get older, your financial responsibilities generally decrease; therefore, so does your need for life insurance. Your goal is to become self-insured—to build enough wealth that you have no need for life insurance.

Choose a life insurance company rated "A" or above.

The A.M. Best Company rates insurance companies in an annual book published for life-insurance industry insiders called *The Best Agents' Guide to Life Insurance Companies;* your local insurance agent or library should have a copy of the guide. Refer to the ratings system in the Best publication, and choose only a life insurance company that's rated "A" or above.

Buy term, save the rest.

Term insurance is simple, no-frills insurance protection—no gimmicks or investments to buy. Therefore, the premiums are the lowest of any form of life insurance you can purchase. If the insured dies within a given period of time, the company **simply pays** the agreed-upon sum of money to the beneficiary. And once a term policy is purchased, future insurability may be guaranteed up to age seventy, ninety, or even a hundred; it all depends upon the company that issues the policy.

Avoid whole life insurance if you can.

Whole life insurance, just as it states, is designed to protect you for your "whole life," but the added security can cost you up to five times as much as "term" for the same coverage. Remember, the goal is to become "self-insured" by having significant assets when you pass, without life-insurance benefits.

Recognize the biggest lines promoting whole life insurance.

When dealing with a crusading insurance salesman, here are some "lines" you'll hear:

"You can borrow the cash value at a low interest rate."

The insurance company is charging you interest on your own money, which you overpaid in premiums—and then it turns around and reduces your *death benefit* by the amount you borrow.

"Your policy will eventually be paid up and you won't owe any more premiums."

A paid-up policy is created only by overpaying your premiums. The overpayment eventually pays your future premiums; all paid-up policies are simply prepaid policies.

"You'll be earning interest on your cash value."

Whole life policies pay an average of only 1.3% interest. Even worse, you never receive it. The interest earned is added to your cash value—and remember, the cash value becomes the property of the insurance company when you die.

"If you buy life insurance when you're young, you'll save money."

It is true that yearly premiums are less when you're younger, but that's only because you will pay greater total premiums over a longer period of time. The only reason to buy life insurance when you are young is to obtain financial protection for your family, not to save money.

The best bet, I think, is to go with term insurance as long as you're saving adequately and building wealth for your "self-insured" future.

■ 3. INSURE AGAINST LOSS, NOT AGAINST FEAR

One of the mysteries of human conduct is why adult men and women . . . are ready to sign documents which they do not read, at the behest of canvassers whom they do not know, binding them to pay for articles which they do not want, with money which they have not got.

—Sir Gerald Hurst

■ SCENARIO
Matt and Jenny have looked around for insurance and have been tempted to insure themselves against everything, including global warming. Problem is their craving for protection could cost them a fortune, "insuring" that they never have a pot to piss in.

Insurance is useful for one thing only: to protect your **assets.** Anything else, under any other name, is a profit add-on. It's tempting to add extra coverages that you don't need "while you're at it," but don't. In most cases, you'll end up wasting valuable dollars that could go into savings.

Don't buy life insurance on children.
The purpose of insurance is to protect against the loss of financial assets. We love the l'il munchkins but they generally are not financial assets.

Never buy whole life insurance as an investment.
Buy insurance for insurance, buy investments for investment purposes. Keep the two separate, and you'll fare significantly better over the long run. An investment company's mutual funds are a better option than those offered through insurance policies—plus, you'll save on fees.

Don't get "frightened" into your life insurance.

A life insurance policy can be canceled by the company only for nonpayment of premiums; therefore, salesmen often use the threat of future uninsurability to get you to buy an outrageously overpriced policy. Here's the truth: about 97% of all insurance applicants are accepted; approximately 5% are charged extra because of poor health. Let's face it: all insurance is a bet, and in the case of insurability the odds are overwhelmingly on your side already.

Raise the deductibles on your automobile policy to $500 or more.

You'll save money by having the higher deductible. How often do you get in an accident? If you do, cough up the extra few hundred bucks for the higher deductible. Don't bet against yourself.

Never file an insurance claim for under $500.

Wise policyholders simply do not file small claims. The insurance company can and probably will raise your premiums next year or, worse yet, cancel your policy. The insurance company's administrative cost of processing even the smallest claim is over $400, and these costs are added to the premiums you pay for lower deductibles. Save your insurance claims only for the big losses.

Avoid insurance gimmicks.

These profit incentives are way overpriced; you'll usually never need them anyway. Watch out for:

Extended warranties on	stereos, TVs, VCRs, appliances
Auto service contract on	all loans, personal or business
Auto service contract on	auto purchases
Credit life on	all loans, personal or business
Credit disability on	all loans, personal or business

The whole idea behind wise insurance buying is to insure yourself against the "real" loss of an **asset**, not a "perceived" loss based on fear. The latter products are designed as profit products to the insurance company.

It's a Wonderful Life:
Smart Investment Moves

Matt and Jenny, having accumulated life's every appliance, seek to sidestep financial lethargy.

■

There is no security in this life. There is only opportunity.

—Douglas MacArthur

■ 1. KNOW THE MARKET BASICS

Mediocre minds usually dismiss anything which reaches beyond their own understanding.
—**François de la Rochefoucauld, French moralist**

■ SCENARIO

Matt and Jenny are ready to begin doing some substantial investing. They've been keeping up with the financial news and have tried to learn as much about the markets as they can. They watch nightly as the day's trading news is recapped, and as exciting as it sounds, they feel confused by much of what they see: stocks making "all-time" highs, others getting crunched, "junk bonds" on the brink of default, and others paying record dividends. They've heard about warrants and options, share buybacks, and stock splits, which only add to their confusion; as soon as they get a handle on the "lingo," another term seems to pop up in the news.

Most of the investment concepts you'll need to know are summarized by the two main categories of financing:

STOCKS, which represent equity (ownership) in a corporation
BONDS, basically IOUs with interest; loans made to another party (loanership)

Under these categories, you'll find a slew of different "vehicles" that are tailored to suit specific needs. In the case of stocks, you'll mostly see *common* and *preferred* stock. With bonds, you'll be exposed to *treasuries* (T-bonds, notes, and bills), which are used to finance our government, *municipals* (state, county, or project issuers), and *corporate* bonds (ranging from AAA to junk bonds in quality). From time to time, you may see "hybrid" instruments that are a combination of these two main forms of financing (like convertibles and some preferred issues).

Even though it may seem like a lot, the reality is that once you understand the basics, the more sophisticated securities aren't that difficult to decipher.

Below, we'll discuss four main investment terms—about all you need to know to be a successful investor. The four market basics are:

1. ### Stocks (ownership)

   I'm pretty sure it was Will Rogers who said, "Buy some good stock. Hold it until it goes up . . . and then sell it. If it doesn't go up, don't buy it!" A stock is nothing more than a certificate of ownership of shares in a company. Some companies are good investments to own, others not so good. **Ultimately, however, the price your shares are worth is what someone will pay you for them,** based on supply and demand.

2. ### Bonds (loanership)

   A bond is the opposite of a stock. It does not represent ownership, but rather an obligation (on the part of the borrower) to repay your invested amount at some predetermined point in the future, usually accompanied by a specified interest rate for the life of the bond as well. Consequently, bonds vary in quality, return, and duration, as well as risk.

3. ### Mutual Funds

   By definition, a mutual fund is a managed portfolio of securities. For our purposes, it is a diversified collection of stocks or bonds—or a mix of the two. In a mutual fund, you don't decide what stocks (or bonds) to buy or sell; a portfolio manager does that for you. The manager will take the money you deposit into his fund and distribute it according to the style and investment parameters of the fund. This allows you to diversify your investment among many different holdings without the inconvenience and expense of buying a few shares of many different companies. You'll pay a management fee for the professional advice and trading, but it's still the smartest and most convenient way to participate in the financial markets.

   Most people are better off in mutual funds, because diversification is the simplest way of reducing risk in your portfolio. Also, selecting which stocks will go up and which will go down is tricky business. If you are long-term oriented, you may do very well picking a few good companies and sticking with them. But if you're like most people, it's better to let a professional manage your equity investments for you through a mutual fund; they usually beat novices year in and year out.

4. *The Dow Jones Industrial Average*
The Dow is an average of thirty of some of the largest industrial stocks in the country, and is widely used as an indication of the market as a whole. **The Dow is an important index** (although there are others, like the S&P 500 and the NASDAQ) **because it contains some of America's oldest publicly traded companies,** such as AT&T, Eastman Kodak, Merck, Coca-Cola, Exxon, Disney, and Mc-Donald's. Consequently, all of the Dow components are considered "blue chips" because of their strength, stability, and staying power.

This index is considered to represent the market as a whole; however, the volatility of the market is of little importance to the investor—unless you own all thirty stocks. The only direction that really matters is the rise and fall of the value of *your* investments.

No man really becomes a fool until he stops asking questions.
—**Charles P. Steinmetz, American electrical engineer**

■ SCENARIO

Matt and Jenny have been interviewing financial advisers, which is not the most comfortable experience. They have taken home piles of literature and graph-filled proposals, which has left them feeling completely overwhelmed. They aren't sure which adviser or program is best for them. Heck, they don't even know what to look for or what questions to ask.

■ EXERCISE

A. SMART QUESTIONS TO ASK **YOURSELF** *BEFORE MAKING ANY INVESTMENT: I have found a few questions that seem to help my clients get clear on their objectives before making any investment. Before each decision you are contemplating, ask* **yourself** *these questions and share them with your adviser. Write the answers in your notebook.*

1. What is my time horizon?
2. What is my target return on this investment?
3. Do I want to buy low and sell high, or buy high and sell low?
4. How many months of negative return am I willing to withstand to achieve my goal?

Whenever you consider selling or making any changes to this investment, open your notebook and review your questionnaire to make sure you're acting in accordance with your original objectives. **If you start to feel the**

urge to make some changes, and you don't know why, go back to your questionnaire.

B. SMART QUESTIONS TO ASK **YOUR FINANCIAL ADVISER**
If you're just now interviewing advisers, you'll want to ask your adviser a few questions as well:

1. **What is your market philosophy or investment methodology?**

   If you share the same ideals, you may have the beginning of a very supportive relationship. If your views differ, look for another adviser. You can't expect them to change their outlook, and with this type of fundamental difference, you'll never be one of their favorite clients. If you ask about their methodology and it's apparent they don't have one or they answer with a "huh?"—run, don't walk, out of their office and find someone else.

2. **What has your track record been over the last one, five, and ten years?**

   If it's below the market averages (11–12% per year), look elsewhere.

3. **What kind of experience do you have in the investment profession?**

   Don't shun anyone just because they're young, but make sure they're *qualified.*

4. **Where do you have your money invested now?**

   Where *they* invest is the most important indicator of their philosophy. If they don't have any money to invest—well, you know what to do.

   C. And, of course, you'll want to ask yourself one question about what *you* want from your adviser:

What are my priorities, by rank?   __Performance
                                         __Service
                                         __To feel good, decisive,
                                             or savvy

If your priority is performance, then you should think long term, disregarding daily fluctuations. If your priority is service, then you want someone to be there to hold your hand when things are tough or return your calls immediately and help you understand your monthly statement. If your first priority is to feel savvy or decisive, like a market player, then you may have the need to call your broker or trade every day—probably not the best way to achieve optimum performance.

One other tip: if you're trying to find an adviser, it's a good idea to set up three appointments in one day (say, at 10:00, 2:00, and 4:00). That way, their different suggestions and proposals will still be fresh in your mind. Let them each know that you are meeting with other people, but you are serious and that you'll be back in touch with a decision in exactly one week. Then do it. One week is plenty of time to make such a decision. Any more time and you'll be likely to forget or delay the decision even longer.

To Do:

- Determine your investment priorities.
- Choose a financial adviser.

■ 3. INVEST MAINLY THROUGH MUTUAL FUNDS

Wealth to us is not mere material for vain glory but an opportunity for achievement and poverty we think it no disgrace to acknowledge but a real degradation to make no effort to overcome.

—Thucydides, 413 B.C.

■ SCENARIO

Matt and Jenny's eyes are temporarily crossed from reading the rows and rows of stock prices listed in their local newspaper. They want to invest and make the right decision, but with all the jumbled numbers and stock and bond quotes, they don't see how they can even decipher enough information to make a choice.

Today, the investor has a tremendous ally—**the mutual fund.**

A mutual fund is a group of several stocks, bonds, or money market investments that are all managed by the same company. When you invest in mutual funds, you own a small share of the fund's entire investment portfolio. Mutual funds give you the *benefits* of a diversified portfolio of stocks, bonds, or money market instruments, *without* the risks, costs, or required expertise of investing in individual issues.

One thing I've found: **the benefits of mutual fund investing make such a strong case that there is virtually no substantial reason to invest in individual stocks or bonds.** But don't just take my word for it, here are some logical reasons to **invest mainly through mutual funds:**

1. **Professional Management.** Mutual fund managers are among the most knowledgeable financial people in the country. You don't have to worry about choosing the stocks, bonds, or other investments; a full-time professional is responsible for doing so.

2. **Diversification.** A mutual fund is a group or portfolio of many stock, bond, or money market instruments that are all managed by the same company. As an investor, you own shares in the entire portfolio. And because of the phenomenal diversification, a mutual fund investment is almost always mathematically safer than investing in any single stock or bond.

3. **Performance.** The track record of every mutual fund is a matter of public record. All you have to do is check your newspaper for the previous day's closing price (which is the net asset value per share), just as you would for a stock. (On the other hand, there is currently no effective way to evaluate stock brokers, financial planners, or investment counselors.)

4. **Income.** You can choose to receive periodic income payments from most any mutual fund.

5. **Liquidity.** You can withdraw part or all of your money and receive it within one to five days.

6. **Investment Options.** Through mutual funds, your investment options are almost limitless. For example, you can invest in stocks, bonds, money market instruments, or overseas companies.

There are several reasons to avoid buying individual stocks and bonds. Purchasing 100 to 1,000 shares of a stock, or pumping $1,000 to $25,000 or more into one or two bond issues, is *eight times riskier* than investing in stocks and bonds through mutual funds. Furthermore, buying individual stocks and bonds means you must pay commissions when you buy or sell.

Mutual funds are the best alternative for small investors. They're easy, convenient, and you can begin for as little as $250–$500. They work great within IRAs or other retirement accounts, and some fund companies will even deduct the money from your checking account every month if you wish.

■ 4. CHOOSE THE RIGHT MUTUAL FUND "CLASS"

The essence of knowledge is, having it, to use it.

—Confucius

■ SCENARIO

Matt and Jenny are sold on mutual funds. They know they'll have to decide which fund(s) are appropriate for them, but now they find that they'll have to make an additional decision regarding which class of fund they should choose—which will affect their costs, the way they purchase their investments, and what level of service they can expect.

Mutual fund companies often offer several class choices for each of their funds:

1. Load Mutual Funds

Load mutual funds are those that charge, say, 3%–9% commissions paid from the money you invest or withdraw. If it is a front-end load, you pay commissions at the time you invest, which reduces your principal. A back-end load means you pay commissions when you withdraw your money, which reduces your earnings. These load funds are usually sold through brokers or financial consultants, so you should expect a certain level of service for your money.

2. 12b-1 Funds

12b-1 funds are mutual funds charging an extra 1% (or so) per year to offset marketing costs but are otherwise no-load. With these funds, 100% of your money is invested and the 1% fee is deducted from the earnings, over time.

3. No-load Funds

These are funds that have no sales fee because they are sold on television or through other means, thereby avoiding a commissioned representative. They rely on the fund's management fee for their profits. No-load funds seem like the way to go, but remember: **you don't invest in a fund to keep your expenses down; you invest to make money.** If you don't need the service or advice, and the fund's performance is up to par, no-load may really be the way to go for you. Keep in mind, however, if you need quick advice, you'll probably be chatting with a phone operator in Des Moines.

![] 5. BLEND YOUR LIQUID INVESTMENTS INTO A PORTFOLIO

Remember that money is of a prolific generating nature. Money can beget money, and its offspring can beget more.

—**Benjamin Franklin**

![] SCENARIO

Matt and Jenny are into giving mutual funds a try, but they aren't remotely sure about how to construct a portfolio. They know they need a mixed bag of different investments for prudence sake, but are totally confused about where to begin.

Basically there are three types of *liquid investment options* for your savings dollars:

Stocks (and stock mutual funds)

Bonds (and bond mutual funds)

Cash (CDs, money market funds, and equivalents)

All three serve different investment purposes for the investor and the issuer. Because the risks associated with each instrument vary, they have historically offered graduated levels of return. Over the years, stocks have more than doubled the returns for cash and bonds. For the stock (and stock funds) investor, that translates, over time, to more than ten times the net worth creation power as the bond or cash investor.

It's wise, however, to have a blend of these three investment types. You may need some help here from a professional, but I'll offer some basic portfolio-building guidelines:

If you are	Your portfolio might be blended like this:
a young turk	*60% stock funds/35% bond funds/5% cash*—to maximize growth
an aging boomer	*50% stock funds/45% bond funds/5% cash*—for conservative growth
driving a land yacht	*35% stock funds/60% bond funds/5% cash*—some growth, but more income
an old fart	*80% stock funds/15% bond funds/15% cash*—to maximize income

As you grow older, or your situation changes, you'll have different objectives for your portfolio. If your objective is to draw every dollar of income you can from your portfolio, you might want to be 100% invested in bonds or other interest-bearing instruments. On the other hand, if your objective is to maximize growth, you might want to be 100% invested in stock mutual funds.

As your objectives shift over time, your portfolio should be adjusted as well. You may want some growth and some income out of your investments. So, a good way to build a solid balanced or mixed portfolio is by diversifying your investments by asset class: stocks, bonds, and cash.

The analysts of most major brokerage firms make asset allocation suggestions that maximize return while minimizing risk. This rational, mathematical approach works well for institutional accounts that manage money with less emotion. However, with individual accounts, it seems that no matter how logical the approach, people still go with their gut feelings when it comes to making money decisions. I'm not saying that's right or wrong. The point is that if everyone on Wall Street recommends being 90% invested in stocks, but you lose sleep with that much money in the market, don't do it.

■ 6. HARNESS THE POWER OF DOLLAR COST AVERAGING

The great man is the man who does a thing for the first time.
—**Alexander Smith, Scottish poet**

■ SCENARIO

Matt and Jenny are excited about contributing to their mutual fund investment program, but they don't have a lump sum to invest right now. They've considered waiting until they have accumulated a significant amount before moving forward but aren't sure if that's the best strategy. Should they add a little bit each month? Or are they better off waiting until they can plunk down a big-figured check?

Here's a turn for us good people of the world: **there's a strategy for investing that actually favors the small investor over the big player**—dollar cost averaging.

Dollar cost averaging is a method of investing whereby you invest a **fixed amount of money at regular intervals,** *over time.* For example, instead of investing $15,000 today and hoping you bought low, you can invest, say, $300 every month for the next four years. You can invest weekly, monthly, quarterly, or yearly—any interval will work as long as it's **consistent.** This strategy works especially well if you're starting small, say, $100–$300 a month, since you can invest a little bit as you get paid. Plus, you'll be investing your monthly savings into a mutual fund, instead of drawing paltry interest from a bank as you wait for the balance to grow large enough.

One of the biggest fears most of us have, concerning our nest egg, is that of investing in the market at the wrong time. Nothing is more discouraging than buying a stock, bond, or a mutual fund just before the market gods decide it's time for a drop in prices. Even a tiny price drop can dampen your spirits; after all, you gave up a lot to make that investment.

The fact is markets do fluctuate. But **dollar cost averaging** works wonders in eliminating most of that fluctuation. The strategy is designed to let you profit in up, down, sideways, and volatile markets. It works because you're buying more shares in down markets at the cheaper price. In most cases, you'll need a full market cycle (about five years) to get the full benefit of this strategy.

So run the numbers for yourself. If you think you're at a disadvantage because you don't have a huge investment portfolio, you're not. **Over time, dollar cost averaging is probably the most powerful tool you can have at your disposal.**

Long-term investing and dollar cost averaging don't entirely eliminate the need to consistently monitor your investment portfolio, however. Just use this tool as a part of your investment philosophy and discipline. In most cases, just practicing a good discipline, like dollar cost averaging, can help you avoid costly mistakes.

7. USE THE BEST-KEPT SECRET ON WALL STREET: THE TOP TEN METHOD

People tend to complicate something in direct proportion to its importance.
—**Michael O'Higgins, author of *Beating the Dow***

■ SCENARIO

Matt and Jenny have learned quite a bit about investing, the paramount lesson being that everyone has an opinion, but no one really knows. They've talked with bankers and brokers and have heard a ton of ideas, but not one that makes terrific sense. Each guru they question seems to have their own method, all of which requires that they must totally rely on the guru for advice and recommendations. Our couple has also stumbled across a simple investment method, the Top Ten Method, which claims to have outperformed the best and brightest in the investment community. Should they take matters into their own hands? Or are they forever at the mercy of gurus who are supposedly in the know?

In the next few pages I'm going to share with you a summary of the single best stock market investment method I've seen. The reason it's such a secret, I think, is this: **using this method, you can achieve better results than most of the pros, with only *one minute* of homework per year.**

The Philosophy

As the most popular market index, the Dow Jones Industrial Average (DOW) is a weighted average of thirty of the largest and most profitable companies in the world. You probably recognize most of the steady companies that make up the Dow; they're household names.

The "Blue Chip" 30 Dow Industrials—A sample listing

Allied-Signal	Disney	IBM	Procter & Gamble
Alcoa	Du Pont	International Paper	Sears Roebuck & Co.
American Express	Eastman Kodak	Johnson & Johnson	3M
AT&T	Exxon	McDonald's	Travelers Group
Boeing	General Electric	Merck	Union Carbide
Caterpillar	General Motors	J. P. Morgan	United Technologies
Chevron	Goodyear	Philip Morris	Wal-Mart
Coca-Cola	Hewlett Packard		

Together, these thirty companies employ nearly five million people worldwide, have combined assets of over a trillion dollars, and combined sales that exceed the gross national product (GNP) of every country in the world except the United States, the former Soviet Union, Japan, and China. To me, it just makes sense to select a portfolio from these quality issues. So, our initial philosophy is that of **regarding the Dow issues as our total investment universe; we'll only consider investments from within this index.**

The Method

Our portfolio selection method is based on the following premises:

1. Common stocks are the smartest long-term growth investment alternative.
2. Dow stocks are enormously important; **all** tend to make good **long-term** investments.
3. A portfolio of out-of-favor Dow stocks could be constructed (allowing minimal risk) that could outperform the Dow as a whole—a feat that has eluded the majority of professionals.

Q: How do we decide which stocks to select out of the Dow?
A: The Top Ten Method simply uses one indicator of value—YIELD.

Q: How does that work?
A: First let me explain the concept of dividend yield, or just *yield,* as we'll refer to it. Most companies in the Dow (twenty-nine out of thirty at this time) pay a return to their shareholders in the form of a **dividend,** which

usually comes from the company's earnings. It can be $1, $2, or $5 per share, or more, or less. But the dollar value doesn't matter that much. What's important is the dollar value of the dividend *as it relates* to the company's share price. **This relationship is expressed as a percentage called the dividend *yield*.**

For example: Let's say that XYZ Company is trading for **$20** per share, and the dividend they pay to the shareholder is **$1** per share. Regardless of how many shares you own or how much money you have invested, your percentage return, on dividends alone, would be **5% (1/20 = .05)**. That's clear enough, right? On the other hand, let's say that XYZ Company has dropped to **$5** per share, and the dividend they pay to the shareholder is still **$1** per share. Now your percentage return, on dividends alone, would be **20% (1/5 = .20)**. Clear again?

The point I need to communicate is this: **There is an inverse relationship between yield and price.** As the share **price** moves up and down the **yield** fluctuates equally in the opposing direction, like a child's seesaw: **when the yield is down, the price is up; when the yield is up, the stock is down.** We use this mathematical relationship to our advantage and **buy only those companies with high yields** and consequently, relatively **low prices.** It's like discount shopping. Choosing a portfolio of ten high-yield/low-price stocks forces the investor to **"buy low and sell high";** **it's a contrarian approach** that avoids guesswork in knowing when to buy **and** sell.

Portfolio Operation

Three steps:

1. **Buy ten stocks.** Invest *equal* dollars in the ten Dow companies that paid the highest yields in the past year.

2. **Hold for one year.** Long enough for some growth, plus receiving the entire annual dividend.

3. **Repeat.** Then readjust to include this past year's ten highest yielders (only three or four will differ).

Q: Why does this simple strategy work so well?
A: There are two parts to the return a dividend stock investor realizes:

1. **Dividend yield,** which we're maximizing by choosing the companies with the highest yield.
2. **Price appreciation,** which we're likely to achieve by buying the issues that are low-priced.

Together, these two forms of return create a measure of performance called *total return*. **Instead of shooting for one over the other, the Top Ten Method aims to maximize the sum of them both. Neat, huh?**

Also, the method buys out-of-favor stocks. Buy low, sell high is an old idea, but how many people really do it? This system tells you exactly when to sell; after twelve months, you recycle your money back into undervalued securities, based on yield.

Q: How well has the Top Ten Method performed over the years?
A: 1. The **Top Ten Method** has outperformed the DOW sixteen of the last twenty-one years.
2. The **Top Ten Method** has had an annualized return of **16.58%** since 1973—50% higher than the **11.04%** the DOW itself posted.
3. The **Top Ten Method** has **never lost money** over any three-year market cycle.
4. The **Top Ten Method** performs well in up *and* down markets.

By using the Top Ten Method your money would have **increased over twenty-fold in the past twenty-one years.**

That's the method. It is simple, but logical and powerful—and it works, without the gurus. **Most of the large brokerage firms offer a unit trust (similar to a mutual fund) that employs this strategy,** and the charges are substantially lower than they would be if you tried this on your own by buying individual stocks.

■ 8. CHOOSE HIGH-QUALITY BOND ISSUES

Never be afraid to expect the best. Never feel we are unworthy or not justified in having the best. I tell you, this is your heritage. But you have to claim it, you have to accept it, and expect it. It is not demanding too much.

—Maharishi Mahesh Yogi

■ SCENARIO

Matt and Jenny have been hearing about what a great environment it is for municipals and other bond investing. They've heard that most bonds are safe—except junk bonds, they know—but they wonder what sort of security they really offer. Will they be "guaranteed" to get their money back? Is the interest on the bonds for certain?

Bonds and bond funds are wonderfully safe investments for people who cannot afford any loss of principle—even over the short term. Bonds might be a good place to invest if you are saving up for a down payment on a house or a car.

When you buy a bond, you are effectively engaging in "loanership," whereby you lend your capital to the issuer in exchange for their promise to repay, plus a stated rate of interest. Their risk of such loanership, then, is determined by the trustworthiness or creditworthiness of the borrower. Let me explain this risk of bond "loanership" with a silly example:

Let's say you met a total stranger on the street, asking to borrow a $100 bill. Is that a safe bet? Probably not, but it depends on how trustworthy the individual is, and the time until payback. So, in our little example, think of two scenarios:

1. If the stranger wants to borrow it for ten seconds so he can show his kid what Ben Franklin looks like, that may be a relatively safe bet. You might even consider lending it to him if he promises to pay you 10% for the use of the money.

2. If the stranger wants to borrow it for thirty years, you might as well kiss it good-bye.

On the other hand, if you buy a U.S. Treasury bond that matures in thirty years, that's probably a safe bet, because our government will probably be around to pay its debts in thirty years. Will the returns be the same in each of these scenarios—the stranger and the government? No way. Each situation has different risks associated with the promise to repay. The stranger may have to promise you 10% return for the use of your money for ten seconds. The U.S. government may only promise you a 6% annual return for use of your money for thirty years.

The way we measure such payback risk is called a credit rating. In general, with duration being equal, the lower credit rating of the bond, the higher the return. However, it is still the free market (supply and demand) that ultimately determines the prices and rates of the bonds—buying a low-rated bond could get you whacked more quickly if the market turns.

Q: Who issues these bonds?
A: Governments, municipalities, churches, schools, and corporations routinely issue bonds to raise money to fund their operations. The states and governments participate in "reciprocal immunity," whereby the Feds don't tax state-issued bonds and the states don't tax federal bonds. Corporate bonds are usually taxable by both state and federal bodies.

Q: How do I know the "credit rating" of such bonds?
A: Independent advisory services, such as Moody's Investors Service and Standard and Poor's (S&P) Corporation, analyze and grade bonds according to their ability to pay back principal and interest. The single highest rating for safety is "AAA" (S&P) and "Aaa" (Moody's). These are the ratings the highest-quality issuers in the world receive, including the U.S. government. As the rating lowers, so does the perceived credit quality of the bond. The quality ratings continue all the way down to "D" (for default) and any bond rated below "B" or "bb" categories may be considered "junk" and is not usually suitable for the conservative investor.

If you are looking for safety as well as tax-free income, municipal bonds are the way to go. They are considered very safe, second only to U.S. government securities. To be assured you own a high-quality issue, try to **avoid bonds rated below "A" by both services.** Before buying any bonds, or bond funds, ask the representative (and read the prospectus) about the Moody's and S&P ratings.

9. DON'T INVEST IN BONDS WHEN INTEREST RATES ARE RISING

He that won't be counseled can't be helped.

—Benjamin Franklin

SCENARIO

Matt and Jenny have been witnessing the profits made in the bond markets—it's been volatile as of late—and they wonder if they should participate. They know that bonds are primary income oriented vehicles, but also understand that there are significant profits to be made if one just knew how and when to trade them.

If you want to use bonds as high-growth investments, you have to be a well-educated, careful investor. You are entering a whole new area of investing: trading on the margin. You can make a fortune, true, but you can also get hammered.

Here's the lowdown on bond (or bond fund trading): there is an opportunity, I won't deny that. More money trades hands in the bond markets than in stocks, by far. (Wouldn't it make sense that the biggest debtor nation in the world would shuffle more debt around than equity?) But you're playing a risky game when you try to bet on bonds. First off, one of the main forces that moves bond prices is interest rates, second only to credit rating, and interest rates are notoriously unpredictable. Even with AAA-rated Treasury bonds—the safest debt in the world—you can get walloped if rates rise on you.

Here's how it works: if interest is on the rise, many a bond investor begins looking for ways to sell their bonds so they can purchase bonds that pay the higher rates. When they sell these lower-interest bonds—you guessed it—the prices go down, and the holders end up getting clobbered. Most of the bond profits you see investors raking in are due to *declining* interest rates—the opposite happens in *rising* rate scenarios. When interest rates are rising, most any long-term bond will lose 10% of its principal value for every 1% increase in the prime rate. That's not good. (You must remember, even though the bond issuer promises to repay your principal, or face value, at maturity—perhaps years from now—the price the market will pay you NOW, should you want to sell, is subject to the laws of supply and demand, determined mainly by current interest rates.)

To make a wise bond investment, choose maturities ranging from, say, ten to fifteen years out. That way, you'll usually get an optimum rate without being subject to the larger risk of the longer bond: all things equal, the longer the bond's maturity, the more sensitive its price is to interest-rate movements. Your best bond-investment strategy should be to use bonds for their income-producing interest payments and hold for the long term.

If you do insist on trying to capture gains in the prices, due to rate fluctuations, make sure you have evidence that rates are *declining,* not rising.

■ 10. RESERVE ONLY THREE MONTHS' WORTH OF LIVING CASH

The greatest of evils and the worst of crimes is poverty . . . our first duty—a duty to which every other consideration should be sacrificed—is not to be poor.

—**George Bernard Shaw**

■ SCENARIO

Matt and Jenny are concerned about the safety of the investment markets these days. They are somewhat afraid of investing at the wrong time and losing some of their principal. Consequently, they wonder if they should move more money into cash investments, such as CDs or money market savings accounts.

It is a good idea to keep a "savings buffer" of two to three months' living expenses for emergency purposes—**but that's all.** Don't feel like you have to have huge sums of money on the sidelines just in case you need it. Most stocks, bonds, and mutual funds can send you your money within five days, so it makes sense to have the majority of your capital working for you at **all** times.

Sitting on large amounts of cash is a big mistake. Inflation and taxes eat up all of your gains, if not more, and it's a dangerous habit to get into. The false sense of security is hazardous to your wealth. Remember: **use it or lose it.**

■ 11. ALWAYS PLAY DEFENSE

Endeavor vigorously to increase your property.

—Horace

■ SCENARIO

Matt and Jenny have been sitting on losing investments for years, awaiting a "comeback." Now they're tired of rooting for the underdog and wonder if they should just bite the bullet: sell the dogs and move into more promising ventures.

Remember this important rule of investing: **capital preservation should always exceed capital appreciation.** We have to invest with the idea of potential return in mind; however, we must be conservative enough to keep our principals as safe as possible. It takes only one bad year to reduce your performance substantially. If you've had more than three down years, it's time to change your strategy. Hoping a loser will rebound is like cheering for the no-named ensign to return from a dangerous Star Trek voyage—the guy's usually a goner.

Even good performance can be brought to its knees by a few bad years or performance. Let's say your mutual fund had earned you 15% three years in a row. But, because of some bad investments in less-than-promising companies, your fund loses 15% in year four. It doesn't seem that bad, right? Wrong. This one bad year has effectively brought your average rate of return down to 6.6%—which sucks. Worse, just to break even (back to the 15% average you had through year three), you'll need to gain over 55% in year five—which *really* sucks because it's next to impossible to achieve.

Always, always, always invest in quality investments (such as the Top Ten, for example). Sell your losers, if you have them, and go with (and *stick* with) the winners. Playing defense, by keeping your portfolio in tip-top shape, makes sure you're in the right investments when the markets move in your favor. I know it's tempting to root for the little guy (and it's painful to take a loss), but even in the most robust of markets, your dogs won't do as well as quality issues. *Would a strong wind help the limper more than the sprinter?*

Don't get careless and forget to play defense by investing in a risky venture or sticking with a loser. Go with quality.

■ 12. IGNORE WALL STREET'S TECHNO-BABBLE

As soon as you are complicated, you are ineffectual.
—**Konrad Adenauer, German politician**

■ SCENARIO

Matt and Jenny have acquired a new nightly ritual: they sit in front of the financial news on TV with a financial dictionary, desperately trying to understand all the foreign terms spewed from the mouths of Wall Street's elite. They get some, miss some, and laugh at others. Still, they wonder: is mastering this lingo really necessary in order to succeed?

We always seem to want more technology and information to help us make decisions in the area of personal finance. Consequently, Wall Street has obliged by bombarding the public with sophisticated computer trading models and impressive **"market techno-babble."** You know what techno-babble is: that *advance/decline line, point and figure chart, p/e ratio, relative strength* type of talk we hear on TV and from our brokers.

A great deal of this type of talk makes sense for traders and financial wizards. But for most people, it's just downright confusing. Worse, it intimidates hardworking investors and keeps them from ever taking the steps they know they need to take, just because they feel they don't understand what's going on in the financial markets.

The truth is, investing is really simple once you understand a few basics. Learn what you need to know and let the pros have their little "techno-babble" language. Understanding it won't help your returns, anyway.

■ 13. THINK AND ACT FOR THE LONG TERM

There's a good time coming, boys!

—Charles Makay

■ SCENARIO

Matt and Jenny have been itching lately to make an investment switch. They've been positioned in their current mutual funds, which are sound, for over six months now and are beginning to wonder if they shouldn't be "moving and shaking" like the big boys.

I've been exposed to many different investment strategies, vehicles, and packaged securities. Some have track records and are really quite good. Some are experimental. And some are lousy, but sellable. But the fact remains: people tend to want something new and exciting. **Old and boring doesn't seem too exciting, even if it works.**

Every year, new hot-shot money managers enter the scene, and some of them are very good. I've just found that most individuals don't care about being a superstar; they just want a reasonable return so they can pursue other interests. If that's your outlook, don't sweat it. **Many strategies will come and go, and some will work, but the only one that has *always* worked is investing for the long term.** Stick to a consistent, long-term approach and leave it alone, and you'll be far better off than jumping from idea to idea.

Successful investing does not come by knowing which new theory is hot. It is a matter of practicing the fundamentals: getting invested, staying invested, and reinvesting the dividends over time.

14. GIVE SOMETHING TO EVERYONE WHO ASKS

Hope. All I have reserved for myself is hope, but hope is more than enough.
—**Alexander the Great**

■ SCENARIO

Matt and Jenny feel fortunate to be living the life they are. They have their health, all the necessities of life, and are preparing for even better days. They look around, from time to time, to realize just how fortunate they are and wonder if they shouldn't lend a helping hand to others in need. They wonder how it would feel, or what would happen, if they could abandon their own quest for more, just for a moment, in order to purposely impact someone else's life. (Nah! Let's get back to the football game, they decide. Just kidding. Matt and Jenny do the right thing.)

Here's a fact I had to learn the hard way: most of us find ourselves settled into a certain standard of living—a rut, if you will. As hard as we try, we just can't seem to break through to the next financial level. *The reason?* Simple. We're doing what we've always done, expecting different results. Which is lunacy.

So, I'd like you to try something different (pretty please). For the next few days, change the way you look at your interactions with other people. Instead of focusing on what they can give you, start to think about what you have to offer them; **start to give *something* to everyone who asks.**

I'm serious. So many times we don't receive what we want simply because we have paid the fair value in exchange—beforehand. The reason we don't have enough wealth is because we haven't given enough of ourselves. The reason we don't have enough wealth is because we haven't paid the fair price for that luxury—you know what I'm talking about.

Making it a point to **give *something* to everyone who asks** is a wonderful habit to acquire because it takes the focus off ourselves—what we want or need—and frees us up to offer value to other people, which is what they pay for.

Giving *something* to everyone who asks doesn't mean you have to give them what they want—*only that you'll give them something you possess in plenty.* If they ask for some of your time, and you don't have it, at least offer a referral to someone who can help them—or a kind word of encouragement. If they ask you for money and you don't have it to give, offer them a suggestion or a polite gesture or a joke to make them smile. If you pay attention, you can always find that you at least have *something* to give, which means you must be wealthy in that something—it says you must have *more than enough* of that *something;* which is a form of wealth, isn't it?

I'm not going to rail about the positive benefits of abundant thinking, but I'll tell you this: IT WORKS. I don't know how, but it does. After ten years in money and finance, I'd like to think I can at least spot an effective strategy when I see one.

I know, I know, it's airy-fairy and a bit goofy. But what have you got to lose in trying my suggestion? After all, you're not giving something you don't have. You're only giving *something* you already possess in spades, right? (Don't be a wiener. Give it a try.)

15. BE A "TWO-QUARTER" PERSON

We have an infinite number of reasons to be happy and a serious responsibility not to be serious.

—Maharishi Mahesh Yogi

■ SCENARIO

Matt and Jenny consider themselves fairly charitable people. They give a few bucks to the local March of Dimes, and Matt even adopted a child through the mail. They're good people. But, let's be realistic: no one offers them any free lunch. Isn't it naive to go around helping other people?

I don't know where I first heard about being a "two-quarter" person, but I like the notion. What does being a two-quarter person mean? It's simple: if someone asks you for a quarter, you give them two. It's a way of life that say's you're constantly giving more of yourself than is expected. Aren't those the people who we like to be around? Aren't they the ones who seem to always rebound and rise to the top? You know the answers; deep down, you really do.

Being a two-quarter person—at work, at home, in traffic—is really a healthy and fun way to be. (We'd all be lucky to have this reputation.) It's not a big thing, not an obligation. It's just a way of quietly doing more and going the extra distance. If you practice this habit, you can't help but change the way you think about yourself and your money.

Most people really want to give and make a difference, but they don't think they can; they don't think they have enough as it is. But understand, it's not about how much money you have or don't have—your life is so much bigger than that—it's about knowing deep down in your gut that you're enough, that you have enough, and that you're worth enough. The mind-set of wealth is that of abundance, and if you don't have it, you've got to earn it by finding ways to exhibit the abundant resources you already posses. How can you ask for more, when you're still childishly hoarding the gifts that overflow you as it is?

It's this feeling of abundance, on whatever level, that drives you to do more, be more, and have more—so you can give more. It's a commitment to something bigger than yourself; a commitment to the abundant nature of our existence.

Being a two-quarter person says that you're above it all, that you can take a step back and express your good fortune, and that you've learned what wealth is about: taking responsibility to do good. It's that simple, but you have to learn that lesson for yourself—not by hoping and wanting something for yourself—but by **doing** for other people.

Singing in the Rain:
The Don'ts to Help You Keep
What You've Got

Matt and Jenny laugh last. Their bosses and bankers have all met their makers, our couple not owing a cent.

■

If money is your hope for independence, you will never have it. The only real security that a man can have in this world is a reserve of knowledge, experience and ability.

—Henry Ford

◼ 1. DON'T UNDERESTIMATE INFLATION

But remember, a billion dollars doesn't go as far as it used to.

—**J. Paul Getty**

◼ SCENARIO

Matt and Jenny have just come into a little money; Jenny's grandmother gave the two a generous anniversary check. They want to find the perfect use for it and decide to tuck it under their mattress in the meantime.

I wanted to bring this topic up because so many people have Cinderella ideas about what this mysterious thing called *wealth* actually brings. Like we've discussed, wealth and ownership implies, and requires, a certain level of responsibility. Since money has a peculiar way of "flowing" to its source—always seeking its "highest and best use"—wise financial managers have learned that they have to constantly monitor, direct, and maximize their power in order to maintain their wealth.

Like our need for air to breathe, every day our wealth craves to be put to effective use. Otherwise it atrophies, overcome by a powerful adversary called inflation—the continual erosion of your purchasing power. As you've already experienced, through steady price increases on just about everything we can buy, inflation is the bad guy in the money game. But it's only bad if you neglect it, don't understand it, or fail to operate on its principles.

Basically, inflation is your money's way of saying: "Use me for good, let me build and grow, feed me, protect me, or I'll slowly die."

As prices go up over the years, inflation assures that a dollar buys less and less. No matter how much money you have, unless it grows, next year it will buy less; your purchasing power will have deteriorated. The only way to keep up with inflation is to maintain growth of your assets by investing it for profitable gain.

Here's the lowdown: by nature, we want to assure ourselves, usually incorrectly, that it won't happen to us; we want to underestimate the risks of this deadly wealth killer. How many people thought divorce wouldn't happen to them? Or bankruptcy? Or illness or accident? See, by closing our eyes to the facts and risks of life and money, we have effectively been duped into a false sense of security.

Here are the facts about the enemy of wealth—inflation:

Every seven years, our dollar is cut in half (assuming a 5% effective inflation rate, which I believe is low). Do you remember how much you paid for your first car? Your last car? The difference, for the most part, is inflation. (Unless, of course, you drove a Gremlin in high school. In that case, most of the difference is improved taste.)

Real inflation numbers are hard to come by. Our government has little to gain by offering inflated figures, but may benefit by offering low figures. True, the price of a loaf of bread may only have increased at 5% each year. But what about home prices in your area? What about your medical and dental expenses? Or your auto insurance?

Inflation numbers are based on large pools of consumer products. Basically, the government takes a huge sampling of products and services, measures their price increases, then offers up an official inflation figure, which is 4–5%. *True, soybeans and banana prices may not have risen that much, but what if you don't buy soybeans or bananas?* Most likely, the products and services you routinely buy are represented by such a broad survey, but I think your true inflation rate may still be much higher.

Inflation increases as you grow older. Let me explain: as you age, you tend to change the way you spend your money. The fastest-rising prices tend to be for services that you'll need when you're older, such as *medical care, prescriptions, travel expenses, and retirement housing.* To tell you the truth, I can't even find an exact inflation number for the pool of products and services retirees purchase, but my experience tells me that it's at least three times what our government's broad pool of services registers for average price increases.

The only way to beat inflation is to outpace it. Rising prices exist, for many reasons, but the only way to overcome them is to invest at rates substantially higher than inflation's erosion.

■ 2. DON'T "INVEST" IN CDS

If you pursue two hares, both will escape you.

—Greek proverb

■ SCENARIO

Matt and Jenny wise up to the fact that all the money under their mattress is collecting is dust. So they stash it someplace just as comfortable: CDs.

Certificates of deposit have long been thought to be the U.S. investor's best friend. They pay a market rate of interest and they are 100% insured (up to $100,000 each) by the FDIC.

But here's the rub: *there is nothing absolutely safe in this whole world. You get what you pay for. No pain, no gain. A fool and his money . . .* I could wax cliché -ically forever on this subject.

Here's the skinny on CDs: Sure they're guaranteed. Yeah they're safe havens for your short-term savings. **But they are not investments.** The CD rates are always just a "little bit" above our current inflation rate; that "little bit" is almost exactly enough to pay the taxes on your "gain." Do you get what I'm saying here? Don't be fooled. *You will never, ever get something for nothing* (ahh, I am warmed, once again, by the afghan of cliché).

Don't EVER forget this formula:	CD "RETURNS"
minus	- INFLATION
minus	- TAXES
EQUALS	**A BIG FAT ZERO!**

Here's the worst part about the deceiving little devils: even though CDs are guaranteed a fixed rate of interest, the rate changes daily. As an investor, you've got to try and catch the highest rate and "lock in" a rate for a long time. (Once purchased, though, your CDs rates are guaranteed for the life of the contract.) You also may incur a penalty for early withdrawal. Because of this "guessing game," most CD investors deposit their money for a six-month or one-year period and "roll over" the CD when it matures, which means that they'll **never know beforehand what rate they'll get in a year when their investment comes due.** (Remember, the rates can change substantially over a year's time.)

Here's the little boogers' crappiest trait: your bank takes your (CD deposit) money and invests it in . . . what? You think they are silly enough to by CDs? No, no, no, little children. The bank takes your money and invests it profitably; they know they have to outpace inflation.

So take my advice: **don't invest in CDs.** Use them for convenience, liquidity, or safety—but not for investments.

Finally (to beat this dead horse completely into dust), imagine if you were retired and living off the income interest from an unpredictable CD. Your monthly income would be up and down like a yo-yo. No wonder we see so many older people going back to work. Even though you planned to retire, inflation hasn't.

■ 3. DON'T CATCH "RISK-A-PHOBIA."

Expect poison from standing water.

—**William Blake**

■ SCENARIO

Lesson learned, Matt and Jenny cash in their CDs and invest their money where the interest is itty-bitty, but so is the risk.

It makes sense to utilize conservative investment strategies, but a small amount of risk is still going to be present if you hope to achieve growth. So, the worst way to approach any investment is by asking, "Is it guaranteed? Will I get back the same amount of money I put in?"

Are you investing to get back the money you put in? Or aren't you really trying to gain some ground? By developing "risk-a-phobia," the only guarantee you'll receive is that, even if you keep your principal intact, the following years that money will buy less and less and less.

Investing absolutely risk-free may seem, on the surface, like a smart strategy, but it's one of the most common mistakes people make. What we fear is losing our money, yet by not taking some risk we slowly lose some of our precious resource every single day—to inflation.

Let me give you an example: suppose you had ten grand that was burning a hole in your pocket today, and you took it to the bank and invested it in something "guaranteed" (maybe a CD or a money market account). In ten years, what would you have? Your ten Gs, plus some small interest, of course, forgetting the fact that it's ten years later and your ten grand will barely take you to Disneyland. Inflation eats away at your principal every single day. The only way to protect your assets is to put your money to work in some useful venture.

■ 4. DON'T TRADE OR TIME THE MARKET

And w-w-where are the c-c-customers' yachts?
—**William Travers, U.S. lawyer, upon seeing wealthy stockbrokers' yachts**

■ SCENARIO

Tired of payoffs the size of a pea, Matt and Jenny catch the gambling bug. They've heard some of their friends talking about an aggressive "can't miss" trading strategy, and they're intrigued. Even though their "long-term" mutual fund investments are performing excellently, they can't seem to let go of the idea of hitting a home run—just once; then they'll go back to their "boring" (yet successful) strategy.

Let me ask you a question, and please give it a few minutes of serious thought: **of the wealthy people you know, did any of them actually make their fortune trading the stock market?** They invest, yes, but not trade. As you know, there is a huge difference between *trading* and *investing*.

Trading is the act of swapping investments frequently in order to gamble your way into a gain.

Trading is exciting to some people, but it's rarely very profitable. Its strategy requires short-term, risky decision making in which the investor switches investments as often as he changes his clothes. I've studied most of the current hot trading philosophies, and some of them do work—for a time. The problem is that even if they do work, you've got to be right twice—consecutively. First, your timing has to be perfect when you buy. Second, you've got to know precisely when to sell. That's tricky, even for the pros.

The one person who *always* makes money trading is the **broker** who gets a commission for every buy and sell transaction. As a serious investor, forget the esoteric forms of market wizardry and invest for the long term; you'll be better off. Besides, if you can get double-digit returns in a mutual fund, without smoke and mirrors, why bother?

Market timing is the act of trying to get better performance by switching money *in and out* of stocks, from cash to the market and back again. It can seem like a compelling notion, but here's the reality: **predicting the future—any future, including the market's—is futile.**

The key to successful investing is owning positions in successful companies (through stocks or funds) and disregarding the daily fluctuations that cause us to react emotionally. Believe me, I've tried to beat it, but staying invested in a conservative mutual fund is usually the best choice.

■ 5. DON'T SPECULATE IN COMMODITIES, OPTIONS, OR PRECIOUS METALS

There's a surefire way to double your money; fold it in half and put it in your pocket.
—Anonymous

■ SCENARIO

Matt and Jenny have been seeing a nightly TV info-mercial advertising "get rich quick" profits. They've seen "real life" examples and testimonials about the profits that can be made and glossed over the small print disclaimers: "people can and do lose money, past performance is no guarantee of future results, and don't blame us if you end up a sniveling pauper." *They are thinking of giving it a try.*

Commodities are the riskiest of all legal investments. Their drawing card is greed and, on the surface, they can sound pretty appealing. After all, an investor can put up as little as 5% in order to control the *entire* investment. But here's the rub: the average commodity's price fluctuation is roughly 1% per day. So if the investor puts up only 5% (which means he's leveraged by a factor of twenty to one), his money will fluctuate an average of *20% per day.* That's great news if the price goes up, but disaster if the price of the commodity drops. Even a small drop can completely wipe out the investor's capital—and FAST.

Here's something else: when the value of the investment drops below the margin requirement, the investor is required to put up more money or else he'll lose the investment and receive a bill for the difference. These margin calls have wiped out the entire assets of many investors.

Options are very volatile derivative securities that are a dream come true for most gamblers because their value rises and falls exponentially with each tick of the underlying security. They are so speculative and misunderstood that most brokerage firms are required by their legal departments to verify the net worth of the investor to make sure they can handle large losses. They also require you, as an investor, to sign a separate form releasing them from liability, and the Securities and Exchange Commission requires you to read (and sign that you've read) an options disclosure brochure. This type of legal precaution should make anyone a little wary. Don't mess around with options unless you truly understand how they work and have a legitimate hedging concern or conservative income strategy, such as *covered call writing*.

What is an **option?** It is simply a right to buy or sell a specified number of shares of stock at a specified price on or before a specific day. A **put** is the right to sell, and a **call** is the right to buy. When buying options, the investor pays a price for the option, called a premium, which is forfeited if the investor does not exercise the option. What kind of price are we talking about? Generally, the premium is from 2% to 10% of the price of the stock plus extremely high commissions; as you can imagine, brokers love that. And three-fourths of options are never exercised and the investors never see their premium dollars again.

It's worth mentioning that many mutual funds now use options as a hedge against fluctuating prices. If your mutual fund uses options, read the prospectus to make sure they're only hedging or writing calls, not speculating. Or better yet, shift to a conservative stock fund that doesn't try such gimmickry.

Precious metals investing is suitable *only* for the most aggressive investors. There is no shortage of salespeople who will try to convince you that gold and silver are a hedge against inflation. But here's something they don't tell you: inflation hedges are usually investment losers. When adjusted for inflation, the real value of gold hasn't changed in a century.

Most of the riskiest investments are designed to be used in conjunction with other business practices: farmers need to hedge against failing crops or falling prices. Stock owners need to "limit" their risk exposure, and certain investors are concerned about hedging against inflation. But, barring these considerations, commodities, options, and precious metals securities are gambling vehicles. Don't participate.

■ 6. DON'T BUY THE "PHONE PITCH"

If you can't convince them, confuse them.

—**Harry S. Truman**

■ SCENARIO

They resisted the lure of the TV pitch. Can our fearless couple resist the power of the phone? Matt and Jenny routinely receive investment sales calls at home, especially since the day they called the "commodity investor's opportunity hot line" for "free" information. They've been stuck on some list and have heard the widest range of pitches since they saw the "wild thang" pitch a no-hitter. A couple of the deals sounded pretty sweet.

In this day and age, we all do a significant amount of business over the phone. It's a great time-saving device, and once you get to know the reputation of your financial adviser, it's completely appropriate to do most of your business over the phone for convenience to you both.

But that's not the type of phone pitch I'm talking about. Today, there is a burgeoning industry of phone boiler rooms specially created to sell off-the-wall investments, such as:

precious metals	*cellular phone lotteries*
commodities	*industrial grade diamonds*
bids on government land leases	*tracts of land in desolate areas*

I know that at weak moments we can all get pulled in by the lure of easy money, but watch out. The easy money is going to be made by the telephone salesman—at your expense.

Maybe the caller tells you: "I know some information that came from a good source (the president or the housekeeper of the president) and the information isn't public yet"—or some other juicy tidbit. Most likely, the only information that's unknown is whether, or not, the caller can scam you out of a few thousand bucks. *If the deal is so great, why are they making eight bucks an hour calling you? Shouldn't they be plunking down their own cash?* (Ask that to receive a quick dial tone.)

Look, I don't want to sound cynical, but I've just never known anyone who ever did well by following the advice of some "divine kid on the telephone."

These schemes deliver little more than the opportunity to lose your money. Even so, tens of thousands of investors fall for these investment gimmicks every year. Keep in mind, too, that if you really *do* get compromised information, insider trading is highly illegal.

Enough said. Don't do it.

That must be wonderful; I don't understand it at all.

—Molière

■ SCENARIO

By now, Matt and Jenny are pros enough to know that people in the finance and investment world have an ax to grind and will grind it on you, if you let them. They've dealt with bankers, insurance salesmen, and brokers and have begun to feel comfortable asserting themselves. Still, every now and then, they find themselves in uncomfortable situations, cornered and hounded by an aggressive salesperson. Sometimes they wonder if it wouldn't be easier to just fork over their money. These people are persistent and not unconvincing.

We're all salespeople, to some extent. We sell our kids on the idea of playing the "quiet game"; we sell our spouse on what to have for dinner; and we sell ourselves at work and in social circles. It should be no surprise, then, to realize that every financial adviser we meet has something to sell us—their services, their ideas, or their company's products. The problem arises when we fail to understand their motives and intentions; when we forget that they're plotting a way to manipulate us to their way of thinking or action. Below are a few of the lines you might hear from your potential advisers. True to the concept, you'll find my arguments below each as I try to sell you on what I believe is appropriate and wise.

1. "You've got to take bigger risks to make bigger profits."
Only amateur financial advisers believe this. Bigger profits can be achieved with the proper knowledge and action. The Top Ten Method, discussed earlier, can earn you 10–20% per year, fairly safely.

2. **"I've got a good tip on a hot stock."**
Watch out for this one! Hot tips ruin most unaware investors. Contrary to what they would have you believe, stockbrokers are always the *least* informed in a brokerage firm hierarchy. Their hot tips usually lose investors' money.

3. **"Zero coupon bonds are a terrific investment for your children."**
Zero coupon bonds, which make some sense, are sold as investments for tax shelters and children for one reason: it makes a good pitch. The best place to invest your children's dough is in mutual funds.

4. **"Let's make some conservative investments and then take a few risks."**
See line number 1. I repeat: knowledge, not risk, is the key; no risks are necessary for a knowledgeable investor. By using the winning investment strategies in this book, even a novice investor can expect to earn 10–20% per year while avoiding pitfalls and risks.

5. **"It's just not possible to average 10–20% per year safely."**
This is another way of expressing lie number 1, and it's absolute nonsense. Tens of thousands of investors who have followed these strategies for two years or more have averaged 10–20% conservatively. These strategies work for everyone over time.

■ 8. DON'T COUNT ON PENNY STOCKS

Often a dash of judgment is better than a flash of genius.

—Howard W. Newton

■ SCENARIO

What if they didn't have to shell out wads of dough to make a tidy sum? Matt and Jenny have been hearing about some hot opportunities in penny stocks. The idea of buying stocks at what seems like pennies on the dollar sounds great. But they know enough to do some research before flipping open their checkbooks.

Penny stocks are highly speculative securities, usually sold by fast-talking brokers. Generally, a penny stock sells for less than ten dollars per share, and the company that issues the stock publicly will often hype the offering with news about new inventions, discoveries, or technological breakthroughs made by the company. The lure used by penny stock salesmen is that their prospects can double or triple their money in a short period of time. It's an opportunity that simply "can't wait." There is no time for the prospect to think about it or to confer with an adviser; he must act now. This is a common high-pressure sales pitch used by penny stockbrokers.

Know this: with many penny stocks there is as much as a 100% difference between the "ask," which is the price at which the broker will sell the stock to a potential investor, and the "bid," which is the price at which the broker will buy the stock from the investor. In that case, the stock would have to double to allow the investor just to break even. Because penny stock brokerage firms control as much as 95% of the market activity of a single stock, they can manipulate the price. And because most penny stocks cannot be found in the newspaper listings, it is extremely difficult for the investor to determine the true worth of a penny stock.

I have people calling me all the time wanting to gamble on rumors and penny stocks. Their justification is that they'll "play" with just the little bit they can afford to lose. If you feel you have to gamble, go to Las Vegas. Don't invest in a stock no one has ever heard of and probably never will again.

Recently, some of the gambler's favorites are stocks I call "petri dish" stocks. Stay away from these types of speculative issues. They are usually companies with one revolutionary product or drug that will save the world—if it works. These companies are betting their livelihood on this one product and if they succeed, the investor will have a home run. **However, if someone in a lab somewhere drops the "petri dish," the stock's price disappears off the face of the planet forever.** Get it?

Don't be afraid to make a well-thought-out investment; just don't get careless and forget the fundamentals that work.

■ 9. DON'T GAMBLE ON IPOs—
INITIAL PUBLIC OFFERINGS

The first man gets the oyster, the second man gets the shell.

—**Andrew Carnegie**

■ SCENARIO

Matt and Jenny have been noticing ads in the financial papers that want investors to buy their company's stock as it's sold to the public. These first-time offerings seem like potentially rewarding deals and appeal to their pioneering spirit. They wonder, "How could we possibly go wrong?"

Let me let you in on a little secret: When investing, **you're the buyer; they're the seller.**

Now, when was the last time you got a completely straight answer from a seller?

An initial public offering (IPO) is an offering of securities for a company that isn't public yet but will be traded on the exchanges after the offering.

There are two basic reasons that the company's owners would want to sell their company **to you:**

1. **They need capital**, which is the most common reason. Some companies need public investor money in order to achieve their goals.
2. **They want out.** How else do you dump an asset, besides sell it? I assure you, however, the pitch behind both of these motivations is equally compelling.

Lately, some very good companies have gone public and investors have been rewarded handsomely for their faith and support. So please know that

I'm not knocking the idea of bringing companies public or even participating in these offerings. It's a great system and Wall Street provides a valuable service matching the sellers with the buyers.

But having been on the other side of the business for years, I'd like to tell you some things you should know about initial public offerings:

1. Most hot offerings are gobbled up quickly by the large institutional investors. These big money players are usually well informed and can spot value in such an offering. Most small investors get the stock that is left over after the big guys get their share; if there's plenty to go around (which is most likely when you're hearing about it), the demand is probably soft and your shares will probably drop in value immediately.

2. Most of these initial public offerings are sold to the investor "with no commission." It seems like a good deal, and sometimes it is, but there's always an internal fee called the "selling concession" that goes to the broker-dealer or investment bank (paid by the issuer to induce their services). All things being equal, the price of your shares will drop (at the market) by the amount of the selling concession that the firm takes; they always make their money first.

3. Some brokers have a "syndicate index," or an average that they have to maintain in order to get the next hot deal; *they have to sell just as much of a bad deal as they do of a good deal.* Don't misunderstand, they don't always know which are good and which are bad; no one really does for sure. It's just that they all have to be sold just the same. You don't want to be faced with the decision of which one you're getting. I assure you, the pitch is slick for both.

4. Rookie brokers are allocated more shares of the weak offerings than strong offerings. Senior brokers usually get the best offerings in the largest quantity. So, if you are considering an initial offering, make sure you work with a senior broker. Just remember, back scratching goes both ways. Senior brokers can help management out by selling large quantities of cold offerings, too.

Here's the point I want you to get out of this: When you hear someone (inside the company or another interested party, such as a broker) talking up their deal, you've got to realize that **they're selling you.** That's not bad, but you need to know what's *really* happening here. If they've taken time to talk about their excellent earnings on TV, **they're pitching.** Get it?

Still, there are some good opportunities out there and most firms are reputable in their dealings. But, all things considered, it's best for most individual investors to avoid the initial public offering market.

10. DON'T MARGIN OR BORROW ON YOUR INVESTMENTS

The eagle never lost so much time as when he submitted to learn from the crow.
—**William Blake**

SCENARIO

Do Matt and Jenny ever feel like they've made it when their broker makes a seemingly terrific offer—to double their buying power! They were told that their brokerage firm can lend them money against their existing holdings, so they can invest even more. There's a small rate of interest, of course, but Matt and Jenny feel that their brokerage firm must really believe in their investments if they're offering to lend them money to buy more.

One of the best ways to get yourself in over your head in investing is utilizing a brokerage firm's margin accounts. Basically, a **margin account** is an account that allows you to buy more investments with borrowed money, using your existing securities as collateral for the loan. The brokerage firm usually lends you the money at a rate just a few points above the "broker call" rate, which is usually near the prime rate. So, it's very tempting to borrow money at, say, 10% when you think your investment will appreciate at a rate of 15% or 20%. But leverage is a two-edged sword. If your investment depreciates in value, you'll have a loss for a securities transaction that you haven't paid for yet—and still owe interest on.

With a margin account, you're taking all the risk—the brokerage firm isn't taking any, because they hold your other securities as collateral. And they usually limit your buying power, as it's referred to, to the amount you could cover if your complete account was liquidated.

In most cases, it doesn't make sense for the investor to use margin. But it makes a great deal of sense for the brokerage firm because they can sell twice the amount of stocks and bonds—your original account's value times two is their rule of thumb for your credit limit. If your securities decline in value, they can still sell them all off, pay themselves back for the loan, and reduce the account to zero, or below, if necessary.

I've heard brokers liken margin borrowing to taking out a mortgage on a house. The comparison is similar, although ridiculous given the circumstance: **if your home value goes down, you can at least still live in it.**

When trying to convince an investor to buy their recommended stock on margin, I've also heard brokers state humorously, "We like the stock so much, we're going to loan you the money to buy it." Don't fall for it. Stay away from margin accounts.

So that's it; you've come a long way. Congratulations!

You've consumed the material and done the exercises (you'd better have), and now you're ready to apply these principals in your own life. That's great. But as you begin to build the future of your dreams and face down the obstacles that may temporarily stand in your way, I'd like you to remember one thing:

You're in control.

You have the ability, right now, to alter your financial destiny forever. You don't have to settle for reliving your repetition-worn financial script over and over. You can jump to the next level rather quickly, if that's your speed. Or you can take it a bit slower, testing the water and revising your sense of your lifework as you go. Either way, it's sure to be an exciting adventure. The financial tools presented here are more than adequate to steer you toward your ideal future. The new vision you've created for yourself, with your *purpose* and *lifework*, can propel you to remarkable heights. Now, understanding and owning your *values* and *code of virtues* can help you stand taller than ever before. I know, I've been there.

I urge you to make this not the end of your journey but the beginning. Take your new habits and run. Run far and fast, as if somebody were running behind you with his boot poised.

Quiz Show:
Learning to Talk Your Walk

Money terms you just gotta know.

Knowledge is power.
—Francis Bacon

■ 1. INVESTMENT DEFINITIONS

Account Executive A brokerage firm employee who is licensed with the National Association of Securities Dealers (NASD) and who advises clients and handles their orders. Some advisers or personal investment counselors have titles, such as investment executive, financial consultant, or registered representative.

After-tax Basis The means by which an investor compares returns on taxable and nontaxable securities, so the comparison is made on a like basis (e.g., apples and apples, not apples and oranges).

Alternative Minimum Tax The federal tax designed to ensure that all wealthy taxpayers pay at least some tax. It closes any loopholes whereby a wealthy person could "escape" all tax burdens by means of various tax credits and tax-free income.

Analyst A person who studies the securities of companies and industries and makes recommendations to brokerage houses, banks, or mutual fund groups as to whether it is advantageous to buy or sell at any given time. Most securities firms employ analysts, sometimes hundreds of individuals and their staffs, to make recommendations on behalf of the firm's clients. Most brokers or representatives pass on these analysts opinions and are discouraged from forming their own opinion contrary to the firm's "approved" recommendation.

Annual Meeting The meeting held annually by a company's managers when they report to the stockholders and board of directors about the company's progress during the year. Any important company policies are voted on at this time and questions can be asked of senior officers.

Annual Percentage Rate (APR) The rate expressed as a percentage that one pays for credit. By law, any consumer loan agreement must disclose this rate.

Annual Report The published report produced by a company's managers, detailing the company's operations, income statement, balance sheet, and other pertinent information for a given year.

Annuitize To make a series of payments on an annuity. This is the payback method on an investment by which someone has built up capital by investing in an annuity.

Annuity An investment provided by insurance companies whereby an investor may make regular payments to an account in order to save money by building up capital, which then accrues interest. It is a vehicle by which individuals can set aside a certain amount of their income for retirement and other savings purposes, and usually includes a specified death benefit.

Asset Management Account A type of investment account with a bank or investment firm that combines checkwriting privileges, direct debit capabilities, etc., like a bank account, but with investment features such as buying securities and making loans on margin. These interest-bearing accounts are a simple way of combining your investment and cash flow accounts for simplified record keeping and other benefits.

Back-end Load The charge that an investor pays when taking money out or withdrawing from an investment.

Basis Point The smallest basis or aggregate point method by which one can measure the increases in the yields on stocks and notes. For example, 1% is quoted as 100 basis points, .5% is 50 basis points, and so on.

Basis Price The price used for income tax purposes as the basis for calculating capital gains or losses in selling securities.

Bear A person who sells or invests in securities with the belief that the market will soon fall and prices will be low. One who is negative on prices is said to be "bearish" on a particular security or the market as a whole.

Bear Market A period of time in which the price of securities continues to fall, generally due to declining economic activity, expectations, or in the case of a rising interest rate scenario in the bond market.

Bellwether A particular security that investors consider an indicator of the overall direction of the market. IBM has long been considered a bellwether because much of its stock is owned by institutional investors who primarily dictate supply and demand.

Beneficiary A person who receives an inheritance, receives the proceeds from a life insurance policy, will be paid the proceeds of an annuity, is the party for whom a trust is designed to benefit, or is the party in whose favor a letter of credit is set up.

Beta Coefficient The factor used to determine the variability of a stock's price based on its relation to the rest of the market.

Bid and Asked The asked (or offer) is the highest price an investor is willing to pay for a particular security at any given time, and the bid is the lowest price the seller of that same security is willing to accept. The difference is "the spread." For example, a security may be bid and offered at 10⅝ to 10¾. If you're a buyer, you pay 10¾. The seller receives 10⅝. The difference (⅛) usually goes to the market maker in the middle.

Block A quantity of stocks or bonds traded or held to be traded at one time. Usually 10,000 shares of stock and $200,000 in bonds.

Blue Chip A term used to describe a security that has built up a good reputation over the years for profit, growth, dividends, and good management. Blue chips tend to be sound, stable companies that have stood the test of time and adverse market conditions.

Blue-sky Law A law that protects people investing in securities against fraud. It requires sellers of securities to register and provide relevant data pertaining to the investment.

Boiler Room A term used to describe a place where people sell fictitious or fraudulent securities using high-pressure telephone techniques. Most boiler rooms have been dissolved by recent laws and regulatory enforcement, but a few still exist.

Bond In effect, a bond is a type of security that represents a loan being sold. A corporation or government entity sells a bond for a certain amount of money. The entity must then pay interest on the bond to the buyer at regular intervals and then refund the original amount of the bond (or loan) at maturity.

Bond Rating A rating given out by independent investment services (like Moody's and Standard & Poor's) that rates each bond or obligation according to the credit worthiness and likelihood of default of the bond issuer. Ratings consider credit quality of the issuer, their past payment history, and their amount of outstanding debt, among other things.

Bottom Fisher A person who invests in securities whose price, they believe, has bottomed out.

Boutique A particular brokerage firm that deals in only a few specialty securities and that deals with a very few selected clients.

Broker An individual who arranges the purchase or sale of securities between buyers and sellers. As a broker, he or she never takes title to the commodity—in this case, securities—involved in the transactions.

Bucket Shop A fraudulent agency that takes orders to buy or sell securities and then waits for a more financially advantageous time to trade. They then pocket the profits accrued from the time of the order to the time of their transaction. Obviously, these agencies are highly illegal, but some individuals still practice this form of theft "under the table."

Bull A person who invests in securities, or the market as a whole, with the belief that prices will rise. One who is optimistic on the future of certain securities, or the market as a whole, is said to be "bullish."

Bull Market A period in which prices in the market continue to rise; a bull market is usually characterized by high-volume trading and widespread optimism.

Business Cycle A period of time beginning with economic growth, expansion, and high employment activity in the business world and ending with a downturn in business activity involving little growth and expansion and high unemployment.

Buy and Hold Strategy The term for the philosophy of investing whereby one buys a security or securities and holds it/them for a length of time over several years. The strategy requires much less monitoring of one's investments and enables any gains to be considered as long-term for tax purposes.

Buying on Margin To buy a security without paying actual cash for it, by purchasing it through the credit extended by the brokerage firm, generally to a buyer with whom the firm has a long-standing relationship.

Calendar A separate listing of securities about to be sold for each type of investment—government and corporate bonds, new stock offerings, and municipal bonds.

Capital Asset Pricing Model (CAPM) A pricing structure detailing anticipated risk and return on an investment, based on the fact that higher risks usually involve greater returns.

Capital Gain The profit or gain made on an investment due to the positive difference between the purchase price and the selling price.

Capitalism An economic system involving private ownership of businesses and property whereby any profits gained in the operation of the business or use of the property belong to the individual owner of the asset.

Capital Markets A market or organized exchange involving the trading of the aggregate of various debts and equities.

Cash Cow Usually a well-established business whose particular product(s) or service(s) are so well known or recognized and accepted by people in general that they sell well and generate excellent cash revenues for the firm.

Cash Dividend The taxable cash payment given to company shareholders distributed from current or accumulated profits.

Cash Equivalents Securities investments that involve so little risk that they are considered to be the same as cash (e.g., short term Treasury bills or money market funds).

Casualty Insurance The insurance a company purchases, which protects the business against property loss or damage and the liability related to the property.

Caveat Emptor Latin phrase translated as "buyer beware"—it was most pertinent before the Securities and Exchange Commission established safeguards for investors in the stock market system.

Certificate of Deposit (CD) A security involving investment of specified denominations of money with banking institutions on which interest is earned over a specified length of time. Interest rates are usually determined by a factor of the current prime rate.

Certified Check A check issued by a bank for an individual who has paid in cash for its issuance. The check is thereby drawn on the bank rather than the individual's account.

Certified Financial Planner (CFP) A respectable distinction for a person who has completed all the requirements establishing his ability to handle all of the financial needs of his clients: banking, estate, and tax planning guidance, etc.

Certified Public Accountant (CPA) A term for a person who has completed all the requirements establishing his competence in accounting, auditing, and tax preparation for individuals and companies.

Churning To trade securities excessively for a client in a way that offsets any possible gains the client might make on his investments, due to the fees and commissions involved in each transaction. Churning can occur even if the investor makes money if the activity is considered unnecessary and solely for the purpose of generating commissions.

Closed-end Management Company A management firm which manages a fund with a finite number of outstanding shares that are often traded on the stock exchange like any stock. Plenty of good mutual funds are closed end, but their price movements are more a factor of supply and demand than of net asset value (NAV), like open-end mutual funds.

Commodities Certain items traded in bulk on a commodities exchange (such as precious metals, foods, grains, coffee, etc.) in order to make profits, or hedge prices, on the speculation of future prices of that commodity.

Common Stock A share or unit of ownership of a public company (usually involving voting rights); the share can be bought and sold, and its price reflects investors' confidence in the company to make profits and grow.

Common Stock Fund A mutual fund comprised only of shares of various common stocks.

Compliance Department The part of any stock exchange, or member firm, designed to oversee compliance in all mandatory exchange regulations within that exchange or firm.

Compound Growth Rate The rate of return that is figured by taking annual or periodic gains and then calculating the growth rate based on the compounding effect of each subsequent gain. In other words, a return that is not a straight annual, or periodic, percentage, but rather a percentage return based also on the growth of the growth.

Compound Interest Interest earned on an original investment plus the growth from interest-on-interest accumulation.

Contrarian The name given an investor who has a reputation for doing the opposite of what the general investing public might be expected to do, under the philosophy that what is expected to occur by the majority of people won't happen; it will be aborted by the very response to those expectations. The contrarian strategy is an inverse reaction to the general dictates of conventional wisdom rather than an action or inaction based upon overt market activity itself. The contrarian perceives typical investors' responses to business trends as another variable that affects the performance of a given commodity, and makes the final judgment incorporating this additional data, rather than ignoring it.

Conventional Mortgage A mortgage loan with interest and payment terms over thirty years or less on an individual's residence. Usually issued by a banking or savings and loan institution.

Corporate Bond A debt security issued by a corporation rather than a government or municipal authority. Interest is paid in regular installments and the entire original amount is repaid at the maturity date specified in advance.

Correction A movement in the price of a security that is negative and which usually reflects a halt to an upward trend. Corrections are a normal part of the market cycle.

Cost Basis The price at which an asset was originally purchased, or the appraised value of an asset inherited.

Cost-of-living Adjustment (COLA) An adjustment usually added to a wage earner's salary to reflect the economic trends of the times, such as an increase in the Consumer Price Index (CPI) or other such basic indices involving the costs of living.

Coupon The interest rate on a bond that is promised to be paid periodically until the instrument matures.

Crash A devastating effect on economic activity whereby markets are saturated, usually after a period of high inflation; it eventually causes loss of confidence in the economic stability of businesses. The individuals involved in the business climate of the day attempt to "pull in" or liquidate their investments, causing a run on financial institutions.

Credit Insurance For businesses, insurance against abnormal losses on the company's accounts receivable. For individuals, it is the insurance an individual purchases in case he or she dies before the debt is fully paid.

Credit Rating The measurement of an individual's or company's ability to pay their debts, as determined by an investigation of the person's or company's debt repayment history.

Credit Risk The existence of the possibility or risk that a financial debt will not be fully satisfied.

Custodian A person or institution having physical custody of the securities of a client base, be it for an individual, a mutual fund, or a corporation.

Deduction The term used by the Internal Revenue Service that allows an individual, company or institution to subtract an expense, thereby lessening the total amount of income used to determine the amount of tax to be paid.

Defensive Securities Those types of securities that are considered safe investments in that they usually provide a steady return on the investment and do not decline substantially in value.

Deferred Annuity A type of annuity whereby payments to the investor are scheduled to begin after a predetermined length of time.

Deflation The term used to identify a downward trend in the value of goods and services; it is the opposite of a period of inflation.

Demand Deposit A type of institutional monetary account that allows instant access to the funds at any time without the necessity that notice be given beforehand to the custodian of the account.

Depreciation The term used to allow for the amortization, or a scheduled rate of allocation, of the costs of large items, such as buildings or equipment, purchased by a company to offset income for tax purposes. To allocate the costs means that a scheduled amount may be used each year as a deduction or expense in order to lower income tax.

Depression The term used to characterize an economic trend involving steady declines in the costs of goods and services, numbers of individuals employed, business suspension rather than expansion, or general business inactivity.

Discount The amount that represents the difference between the lower price a bond will sell for on the current market and its higher face or redemption value. Conversely, a premium is the higher price a bond will sell for related to its now lower face value.

Discount Rate The interest rate that the Federal Reserve charges its member financial institutions for loans. Since banks set their loan rates above their cost of funds, the discount rate sets a floor to interest rates.

Disposable Income All the funds available to a person or institution after all income has been received and all expenses, taxes, and annual miscellaneous fees have been paid. Marketers like to consider disposable income as that amount of money the consumer is willing to spend on luxury items once their current obligations have been met.

Diversification A philosophy of investing whereby all the investments of a person or institution are not allocated in only one arena. Investing in a variety of different securities or assets allows an internal system of checks against the possibility of total or devastating loss should one particular investment fail or decline drastically in value.

Diversified Investment Company A company that follows the investment philosophy of investing in a wide range of dissimilar securities and/or assets so as to prevent the possibility of financial ruin should one arena of investments fail.

Dividend The funds paid out in the form of money or additional shares by a company or financial institution representing one unit of that person's or institution's share in the profits.

Dividend Reinvestment Plan A plan whereby one's share of the profits of a company or institution are automatically reinvested in more shares rather than paid in cash.

Double Taxation A reference to the fact that an individual's dividends, or shares in a company's profits, are taxable income to the individual while those same funds were a part of the corporation's taxable income as well. In effect, those earnings are taxed twice—once when the company reports them and once when the individual receives those earnings in the form of a dividend.

Dow Jones Industrial Average The calculation of the average price of a representative sampling of thirty actively traded, very safe or blue chip stocks; these averages are published by Dow Jones & Company. The representative sampling includes industrial firms as well as American Express Company and the American Telephone and Telegraph Company. The Dow is the oldest and most revered index, or barometer, of the stock market. The individual companies used to determine the index are changed periodically. The index is calculated by taking the total of the closing prices of the representative stocks for a single day and dividing by a number that is designed to adjust for splits, dividends, and mergers. It is quoted in points rather than dollars.

Early Withdrawal Penalty The term used for the penalty charged against investors in securities of a fixed term if the funds are withdrawn from the investment before the maturity date.

Earned Income The income of individuals, or investments paid by an individual, providing goods and services or a fund generating profit.

Earnings Per Share That per share amount of a company's profits allocated to each outstanding share of common stock. For example, if XYZ Corporation earns $1 million and it has one million shares outstanding, EPS would be $1.

Estate The term used to describe all of a person's financial holdings and assets at the time of his or her death.

Estate Tax The term for the tax that is levied against a person's estate before it is distributed to the heirs of the estate at the time of his or her death.

Exchange Privilege The term used to describe each shareholder's ability or right to move or transfer his money around between the different funds managed by the same conglomerate, providing they're within the same family. For example, Fidelity Mutual might have a whole series of funds designed for different investment needs—one for steady long-term growth, one for high-yield, high-risk growth, etc. If you have money invested in one of these funds, you can either call or write to them, telling them to switch your funds from one type of fund to another.

Family of Funds A grouping, within a mutual fund, of funds that have differing investment objectives but share the same management or investment company.

Federal Deposit Insurance Corporation (FDIC) The federal agency that was established after the crash of 1929 to guarantee funds of depositors in financial institutions ($100,000 per person, or shareholder of an account, per institution).

Federal Funds Rate The interest rate charged by Federal Reserve member banks with excessive funds in reserve at the Federal Reserve district bank to those member banks that need short-term loans to meet their reserve requirements. In short, the Federal Funds Rate is the rate at which Federal member banks loan to each other. This rate is the most sensitive indicator of the direction of interest rates because it is set daily by the market, not by banks and the Federal Reserve Board, as the prime rate and the discount rate are.

Federal Reserve Bank One of the banks of the Federal Reserve system that monitors financial institutions for compliance with the Federal Reserve Board regulations and that acts as depositor for transfers of funds between banks within a region.

Fixed Annuity An investment sold by an insurance company that guarantees a fixed amount of payment to a person for a fixed amount of time once the obligations of the annuity have been satisfied.

401(k) Plan Savings plan allowing an employee to make pretax payments or deductions from his earnings into a company fund in an attempt to set aside money for retirement.

Front-end Load The term used to describe the fees charged an investor at the time he purchases or invests in a security.

Gross National Product (GNP) The term used to describe the status of the economy by measuring the total value of all goods and services produced by a country over a period of one year.

Hemline Theory Imaginary theory that the status of the economy and thus the markets are reflected by the latest fashion; it focuses on the movement of women's hemlines (i.e., shorter hemlines indicate bullish or rising prices, and longer hems indicate bearish or falling prices). This theory is mentioned tongue-in-cheek in business schools with no factual basis other than the observation that fashion tends to play a role in reflecting the mood of the population as a whole.

Index Fund A mutual fund whose investments resemble the broad base of an investment index, such as Standard & Poor's Index, ensuring that the profitability or income of the fund will reflect the success of the market as a whole.

Individual Retirement Account (IRA) A personal retirement account designed for individuals to set aside pretax dollars into a retirement account by investing in a variety of securities.

Individual Retirement Account (IRA) Rollover The term used when a person retires or terminates employment with his company and takes his vested interest in the company pension or retirement fund, "rolling it over" into another form of investment and account. This is done to avoid taking possession of the funds, which would incur taxes on the liquidation of the investment. The term can be used when an individual transfers funds from one retirement account to an IRA account without taking possession of the funds.

Inflation The term used to describe the normal increase in the cost of goods and services; it generally reflects economic growth.

Inflation Rate Rate at which the cost of goods and services increases, as measured primarily in the Consumer Price Index.

Initial Public Offering (IPO) The initial or first offering of a company's stock to the general public.

Inside Information The term used for the information gathered involving imminent corporate moves and/or affairs not available to the public to date and that, if known, would enable individuals to take unfair advantage in making profitable investments involving that company's stocks.

Institutional Investor An organization or financial institution that trades in large volumes of securities, such as banks, investment houses, labor unions, mutual funds, insurance companies, etc.

Internal Revenue Service (IRS) The governmental agency in the United States responsible for administering the rules and regulations involved in collecting federal income taxes levied by Congress and carried out by the Department of the Treasury.

Joint Account An account of funds or securities owned by two or more people.

Joint Account Agreement The basic document stipulating the parties involved in any joint account and containing information relating to them, including an example of their signatures.

Jumbo Certificate of Deposit A certificate of deposit with a minimum deposit prerequisite amount of $100,000.

Junk Bond A bond with a high speculative risk value and therefore a low credit rating. As they are more risky and volatile, they tend to pay higher investment yields.

Keogh Plan A tax-deferred pension account geared for people who want to set aside funds for retirement and who are self-employed or who work for unincorporated businesses.

Life Expectancy The calculated average age that a person is expected to reach before dying. This rate is frequently used by insurance companies as a basis by which they structure their various insurance plans.

Load Fund A mutual fund, sold by an investment firm or broker, that involves a sales charge paid up-front. For the fee, advice and counseling are offered as to any benefits involved in buying more shares or selling shares at any particular time.

Lump-sum Distribution A distribution or payment settling a financial account, usually the liquidation of one's retirement account, in one lump sum. The term "lump-sum distribution" usually applies to liquidating one's retirement account with intent to pay any taxes due, as opposed to exercising the IRA rollover option, which is not a taxable event.

Managed Account An investment whereby one party entrusts the management of the funds or securities involved in the investment to another individual or institution. Managed accounts offer the professional advice and diversification benefits of mutual funds, while providing the investor with personalized service and account maintenance.

Management Fee The fee charged by the manager of an investment account, or mutual fund, for his services; it is usually taken out of the investment earnings before distribution of earnings.

Margin Account An account with a brokerage firm whereby the investor can purchase securities without an exchange of money involved (i.e., the investor borrows the funds used to purchase the security from the brokerage firm).

Maturity Date The date on which a debt instrument matures and the principal amount of the debt must then be settled between parties.

Money Market Fund An investment fund that is comprised of a variety of highly liquid and safe securities and that pays low rates of interest. The share price remains the same and only the interest rate increases or declines, depending on market conditions. Because of this safety and liquidity, money market funds are considered cash equivalents.

Municipal Bond A debt instrument issued by a state or local municipality, usually to pay for special projects or to raise funds for general financial needs. The proceeds or income generated from this investment are exempt from federal income taxes.

Nest Egg The term used in referring to assets or commodities put aside by individuals for retirement purposes.

Net Asset Value (NAV) The bid price or market value of a mutual fund share; it describes the selling price of a share of that particular fund. It is calculated by combining the market share value of all shares in the security with all the assets of the fund, and then dividing the result by the total number of shares outstanding. The market price of most open-end mutual funds quoted in the paper is the NAV.

Net Worth The amount a company or individual is supposedly worth; it is a calculation of the amount by which assets exceed liabilities. For individuals it is calculated by subtracting any outstanding debts from the total of the market value of all the assets owned by the individual.

New York Stock Exchange The oldest and most well known stock exchange in the United States; it is located on Wall Street in New York City.

No-load Fund A type of mutual fund wherein the investment company charges no front-end fee to investors, as the investors buy directly from the fund companies rather than through brokers. Unlike load funds, there is no hired broker or adviser to help you with your decision. With all funds, load and no-load, the investor still pays a management fee to the advisers of the fund. Whether a fund has a load or not has no bearing on how well the securities in the fund will perform. The determining factors are the quality of the fund and its management.

Opportunity Cost The term used to define the cost involved in an alternative course of action taken in an attempt to generate the highest possible rate of return.

Over the Counter (OTC) The term used to describe stocks sold by smaller companies that do not meet the criteria of the listing requirements for the organized exchanges such as the New York Stock Exchange. These stocks are sold through electronic communications connecting dealers with potential buyers.

Penny Stock A stock that traditionally sells for less than a dollar a share, but stocks up to $10 per share can be considered penny stocks because of their reputation for high volatility and unproven track records. They are often traded OTC.

Portfolio The combination of financial holdings and assets held by an individual, institution, or trust.

Prime Rate The current rate of interest charged by banks to their most financially stable and preferred long-standing customers. The rate is usually the lowest marketable rate that the bank can charge and still make a profit.

Profit-sharing Plan A plan set up by a company and offered to its employees whereby the employees share in the company profits. Annual contributions are made by the company and are then invested and disbursed to the employees individually upon their retirement or upon their leaving the company.

Registered Representative An employee of a stock exchange member broker or dealer who acts as an adviser and fund administrator for his clients.

Retail Investor An individual who invests in securities and commodities in order to make a profit for himself and not on behalf of any organization or fund.

Risk Averse The philosophy that any reasonable investor will seek investment in securities that pose the least amount of risk and that he will expect a higher rate of return should he invest in more risky ventures.

Rule of 72 A formula that attempts to derive the time necessary for an amount of money to double in value at a given compound interest rate. One divides the interest rate by 72. In other words, $1,000 will double in value at the compound interest rate of 8% over a period of nine years.

Self-directed IRA An IRA that can be managed by its owner, who designates a person or institution to administer the account.

Spousal IRA An IRA that can be opened by an individual's nonworking spouse.

Standard & Poor's Composite Index of 500 Stocks (S&P 500) An index of 500 blue chip stocks showing their aggregate value in relation to their value during a base period in 1941–1943. The index is comprised mostly of companies listed on the New York Stock Exchange but also has a representative sampling of some American Exchange and over-the-counter companies. The sampling represents approximately 80% of the stocks listed on the New York Stock Exchange, and the actual proportions of companies used include 400 industrials, 60 transportation and utility companies, and 40 financially related firms.

Stock Certificate The certificate or document issued by a corporation in exchange for funds used to purchase a share in that company's stock. The certificate indicates the number of shares owned, the type of stock purchased, and the par value.

Stock Dividend The method by which a corporation or financial entity shares the profits in the form of additional shares of stock rather than with cash.

Stock Exchange An organized institution wherein stocks and bonds are traded in a market by members of the exchange, acting both as brokers and traders.

Stock Indexes and Averages Calculations used to measure the changes in representative samplings of the stock market. The index computes an average in relation to a previous mean level of prices, whereas the average is a computation of the average or mean price of a representative grouping or sample of stock prices.

Taxable Equivalent Yield The measurement of the taxable yield on a corporate bond and the tax-free yield of a municipal bond so as to make the comparison reasonable and consistent with financial gains after taking income taxes into account.

Taxable Income The income figure that is used to calculate the amount of taxes an individual or company must pay; it is derived by adjusting out or subtracting all legitimate deductions from the aggregate of all income.

Tax Bracket The general percentage of tax paid on income derived from taking the total income tax obligation and dividing it by the total income. The tax bracket is also reflected in the area in the tax tables where one finds the actual tax obligation, or multiplier, to compute one's taxable income.

Tax-deferred The term used to describe funds that are currently free from tax obligation until such time as the investor liquidates or takes possession of the funds. An example is the individual retirement account, in which one sets aside funds until retirement and the earnings and contributions are tax-deferred until withdrawal.

Tax-exempt Security An investment or security in which the interest or dividends earned on the investment are not taxable; its funds are usually for the purpose of benefiting a local or state municipality, as in municipal bonds. An entire mutual fund portfolio can be derived solely from such tax-exempt securities.

Tax Shelter An investment from which the funds earned are sheltered from any tax obligation.

Telephone Switching The process of switching or changing investment funds from one type of account to another in or between a family of funds, with the assistance of a representative over the telephone.

Term Life Insurance A type of insurance policy that is designed to give a specified amount of benefit at death and that does not build up any additional cash value over time, in contrast to a whole life policy. As a result, a term life policy is considerably cheaper.

Total Return The calculation of the annual return on an investment; it involves the aggregate amount of the value of the dividends or interest earned on the investment, plus any appreciation in the value of the asset itself.

Treasuries Investment instruments that are debts of the U.S. government with the collateral as one's "full faith" in the stability and continuance of that institution. The interest earned from treasuries is exempt from state and local, but not federal, income taxes. There are three types: 1) Treasury bills, which are short-term securities that mature in one year or less and are discounted or sell for less than face value; 2) Treasury bonds, which are the same instruments issued for a longer period of time, such as ten-year or longer and are of denominations of $1,000 or more; and 3) Treasury notes, which are something in between in that they can have maturity dates of between one to ten years, and they involve denominations of between $1,000 and $1 million.

12b-1 Mutual Fund A type of mutual fund sold directly by the fund administrators so that there are no load costs. The cost of the fund does, however, involve a percentage of the promotion costs in offering the fund for sale to the public.

Underwriter Another name for a company that, in exchange for premiums, sells insurance against the risk of the occurrence of death, theft, loss by fire or illness, etc.

Unearned Income (Revenue) Income from sources that are not wages, tips, etc., such as dividends and interest on investments.

Uniform Gifts to Minors Act (UGMA) A law of most U.S. states that stipulates rules for the administration of the assets of a minor. Included in the law are rules applying to the custodian (a parent or an independent trustee) who takes charge of the assets and invests them for the benefit of the minor.

Unit Investment Trust A type of investment in which a fixed assortment and number of income producing securities is purchased, then is registered with the Securities and Exchange Commission. The Top Ten Method suggested in this text is usually structured as a unit investment trust and offered by many brokerage firms.

Universal Life Insurance A type of life insurance that has the benefits of combined low cost protection against death with a savings and investment plan that involves tax-deferred earnings.

Value Line Investment Survey A service that advises prospective investors or other interested parties on the ranking and volatility of numerous stocks for safety and potential earnings. The survey projects which stocks will perform well over the next year, based on the previous twelve months' performance.

Variable Annuity A life insurance package that includes an investment portfolio of a variety of securities (usually common stocks) and whose value consequently goes up or down depending on how well the securities in the portfolio perform.

Variable Life Insurance A competitive variation of whole life insurance that allows the administrators of the policy to invest the cash value of the aggregate amount of life insurance policyholders in various securities, so as to allow for income producing potential over time.

Variable Rate Mortgage (VRM) A type of homeowners' mortgage loan with a fluctuating interest rate that varies according to money market rates or the administrator's cost of funds over time. Also called an adjustable rate mortgage.

Volatility The potential for the value of a security to substantially increase or decline in market value within a relatively short period of time. One measure of volatility is standard deviation: the variance of probable returns in relation to the mean return of the underlying security. Another is the beta coefficient: the covariance of a security's volatility in relation to the overall market.

Wall Street Originally, the financial district in New York City, where numerous investment and brokerage firms are located, was designated because of its close proximity to the nucleus—the New York Stock Exchange, at 11 Wall Street. Today, however, Wall Street is more an industry than a location. Even though New York is still considered the center of the financial universe, through computers and telephones, a person in California can be just as close to Wall Street as the floor brokers on the exchange.

Whole Life Insurance A type of insurance policy that not only pays a benefit in the event of death but that also builds up a cash value over time. The premium is set for the entire length of the policy and the earnings on the cash value of the policy are reinvested by the administrators to accumulate tax-deferred earnings.

Widow-and-orphan Stock   The term given to a type of stock that is considered very safe and that pays high dividends. It is usually not at all volatile and is usually not subject to the vacillations in price of differing industries in comparison to the overall market.

Yield   The income or interest earned on one's investment. In bonds, the yield involves the rate of return on the bond, the purchase price, the redemption value, the interest rate and the amount of time remaining until maturity. For stocks, this figure depends on the rate of return paid in dividends. It must be noted that as the price of a stock or bond rises or falls with the market, so does its yield rate.

Yield Equivalence   The interest rate wherein tax exempt securities and taxable securities provide the same rate of return. To calculate the yield equivalence, the tax bracket is taken into account for taxable securities and the tax yield equivalence is divided by the reciprocal of the tax bracket for the calculation. For example, a person in a 42% tax bracket wishing to figure the taxable equivalent of a 10% tax-free municipal bond would divide the 10% by 58% (100 minus 42%) to get a yield equivalence of 17.24%.

Zero-coupon Bond   A bond sold at a deep discount in that it makes no periodic interest payments and is redeemed at a higher-than-purchase face value on a specified maturity date. Similar to a savings bond, the value of the security increases with the appreciation of the value of the bond over its original price.

■ 2. INSURANCE DEFINITIONS

Adjuster The insurance company employee whose responsibility it is to assess a claim and determine the amount of money that the insurance company is willing to pay to settle the claim.

Death Benefit The sum of money that is paid to the beneficiary of a will upon the death of the policy holder.

Fees and Commissions The charges added to the cost of insurance policies by the insurance companies to cover their administrative, advertising, marketing, and sales efforts.

Grace Period A period of time in which one may pay the premium of an insurance policy after such time as the premium amount becomes due and payable, and before added penalty fees are incurred or the policy is canceled.

Group Insurance An insurance plan that groups together, for insurance purposes, a number of people who usually have a common base (e.g., they are all employees of the same company).

Hazard A situation that will precipitate an accident or injury due to the presence or occurrence of potential harm or danger.

Incontestable Clause A clause insertion into insurance policies that prevents cancellation of policies after a certain length of time due to misstatements or erroneous information provided by the insured.

Insurance A contract wherein an individual pays a premium or fixed sum of money periodically in return for loss coverage in the event of illness, retirement, disability, death, etc.

Insured The person for whose benefit a premium or fixed cost is paid in return for coverage against potential loss due to illness, accident, retirement, death, etc.

Life Insurance A contract whereby an individual pays a fixed sum of money periodically toward a future benefit for such occurrences as retirement, death, dismemberment, etc.

Mutual Insurance Company A cooperative association that exists for the purpose of insuring its members.

Owner The party who makes payments toward an insurance policy and who may or may not be the beneficiary of the policy.

Peril An unwelcome occurrence against which insurance policies are generally written, such as a severe illness or injury, bodily dismemberment, death, fire, theft, etc.

Policy Term A fixed determination of time during which a particular insurance contract is in effect.

Premium The sum of money paid at periodic intervals to an insurance company in return for coverage against some potential or future occurrence, such as illness, theft, death, or retirement.

Rate The mathematical calculation by which the cost of insurance can be deduced. The total rate would be the cost per every $1,000 unit of insurance.

Risk The potential for a certain occurrence, hazard, accident, or loss. Also the amount that an insurance company stands to lose should a particular hazard, accident, or loss occur.

Settlement Options Different methods by which an insured person may choose to take or receive the benefits of the proceeds of an insurance policy.

Stock Insurance Company A type of company that sells insurance to and, at the same time, is owned by its own policyholders or stockholders.

Surrender Charge The penalty amount or surcharge, stipulated in insurance contracts, that the insurance company may keep should you choose to cancel the policy before it comes to term.

Underwriting The process of analyzing whether the risk involved in renewing an expired insurance policy, or establishing a new insurance policy, should be taken by the insurance company.

Universal Life A type of insurance policy issued not only to provide benefit against the occurrence of death, but also to set aside funds for future benefit, such as retirement, by means of an investment plan.

3. MUTUAL FUND DEFINITIONS

Account The record of your investments with the mutual fund. The account begins when you invest money in the fund. It ends when you withdraw or sell all your interest (represented by money) in the fund.

Adviser Mutual funds need to have someone to whom the managers can turn for advice. This is the function of the adviser. Simply, they advise the people managing the fund. An adviser is usually an individual, but oftentimes can be an organization such as a bank.

Aggressive Growth Fund The philosophy of a fund, as determined by the fund's managers, to invest primarily in securities involving volatile or risky techniques in an attempt to make high profits quickly.

Asked Price The price tag on the commodity (the fund) that you are buying, similar to the price tag on shoes or clothes that you buy. This figure represents the value of the asset (the fund) at the present time. It may go up or down depending on the fund's performance.

Asset Management Accounts Funds that allow the benefits of a checking account such as check writing, direct withdrawal cards, and the electronic ability to transfer funds.

Bid Price When you want to sell your interest (shares) in the asset (the fund), you have to sell it back to the people managing it. They offer you a price for it, the bid price, which is the value of the shares less any fees they receive.

Capital Gains Distributions If the fund is not a tax-free fund (made up of municipal bonds, etc.), then any gains or earnings are taxable. The fund managers will let you know by year's end (i.e., in time for taxes) what your share of these taxable gains is so you can record this information when you file your annual income tax return.

Capital Gains or Losses If the value of the fund goes up after you buy it, you make a capital gain. If the value of the fund goes down after you buy it, you have a capital loss. In addition, the people managing the fund buy and sell investments; if they sell for more than they bought, the fund has a capital gain. If they sell for less than they bought, they have a capital loss. The fund managers will inform you of your share of these gains and losses for tax purposes.

Cash Position The managers of the fund are constantly buying and selling stocks and bonds. The cash position represents the accumulated money belonging to the fund between investments or the amount they've allocated for cash reserves.

Certificate A fancy printed document showing that you own shares in the fund. It is very similar to a marriage certificate. Like currency, it is printed in such a way as to make it difficult to forge. Generally the fund managers do not mail you the certificates. Most funds' records are kept on elaborate computerized databases maintained by the managers of the fund.

Distributions Your share of the moneys earned by the fund. The managers can offer you either the cash value of these earnings or the equivalent in additional shares in the fund.

Dividends Distribution A dividend is your share of the earnings produced by the fund and not reinvested. The managers declare the dividend and then distribute this according to the number of shares (or the amount of interest) that you hold. The greater the amount of interest you have in the fund, the greater your dividend will be.

Equity Income Funds The philosophy of a fund, as determined by the fund's managers, to primarily invest in securities involving equity income first and growth second.

Growth Fund The philosophy of a fund, as determined by the fund's managers, to invest primarily in securities involving a steady, good growth potential—as opposed to, for example, high-yield or income-producing investments.

Growth and Income Funds Funds whose managers attempt to give investors steady growth and steady income at the same time. The managers invest in stocks priced in the lower ranges so that any yield involves a higher percentage.

Insured Money Market Fund Funds that are insured against loss. The insurance premium is paid by the interest income of the fund.

Management Company The people hired to manage the fund. These people handle all the transfers of monies in and out of the fund and between funds.

Money Market Mutual Funds Mutual funds whose managers invest in securities that have maturity dates of a year or less and are extremely safe as well as interest-bearing. Their performance is dependent on current interest rates.

Mutual Fund An investment fund administered by an investment firm that pools money from investors and invests it in a diversity of securities, and that can thereby offer the security of diversification and professional management.

Net Assets The accumulation of monies in a fund over and above any liabilities or debts or equity.

Net Asset Value Per Share (NAV) The amount of money each share is worth after computing the monies the fund has accumulated, less any liabilities or debts. This net asset value (NAV) is divided by the total number of shares; the result is the per-share net asset value price (equity per share).

Payroll Deduction Plan Similar to an automatic savings plan. An employer automatically deducts a specified amount from your paycheck to be sent directly to the fund.

Performance The calculation of how well a fund is doing by measuring the percentage increase in its value over time.

Portfolio All the stocks, bonds, and other miscellaneous investments accumulated by a fund.

Portfolio Turnover The calculation of the percentage of the fund's investments that were sold and reinvested during one year.

Prospectus The fact sheet published by the managers of the fund, describing the philosophy of the fund and its management parameters (e.g., low risk, high risk, which securities are invested in, etc.). The prospectus describes the procedures involved in buying and selling, as well as the fees charged and commissions earned by the manager.

Reinvestment Privilege Instead of having your investment earnings sent to you by check, you can have your earnings reinvested in the fund, which increases the number of shares you own. This is the best choice for investors wanting growth of their portfolios.

Specialty Stock Mutual Funds Certain mutual funds that are not for the average investor but designed around the more experienced investor. Examples of some of these funds are:

  Option Fund: a fund whose managers buy stock options—or the right to buy and sell certain shares of stock at a fixed price and date.

  Index Fund: a fund whose content is made up of the majority of stocks in the Standard & Poor's 500 or other index. The performance result of the fund is the same as that of the index it mirrors, less any fees.

  Balanced Fund: the type of mutual fund whereby the managers attempt to buy securities such as common and preferred stocks, bonds, and other securities in order to obtain the highest rate of return without a high-risk factor.

  Clone Fund: a newly created fund that closely resembles a fund already in existence in a family of funds.

  Closed-end Fund: a fund whose makeup is comprised of a fixed number of shares that are traded on the stock exchange.

  Social Conscience Fund: a fund that invests in organizations that exist primarily for social good.

  Industry Fund: a fund that owns stock in only one industry. The stocks perform as well as the industry in which the funds are invested.

  Sector Funds: a fund that focuses on securities in certain industries, or sectors, that the manager believes will outperform the overall market.

Emerging Company Growth Fund: a fund whose managers invest in securities involving newly emerging companies with potential for future growth.

Precious Metal Fund: a fund whose managers invest mainly in mining companies whose main purposes are to extract gold, silver, platinum, and other precious metals from the earth.

Multi-fund: a mutual fund whose managers invest mainly in shares of other mutual funds.

High-yield Fund: a fund whose managers invest primarily in corporate bonds with high interest rates and usually low ratings.

Fixed Income Funds: a fund whose managers invest primarily in long-term bonds, seeking a main objective of steady income.

GNMA Fund: a bond fund whose managers invest primarily in government national mortgage bonds.

Tax-exempt Money Market Funds Funds whose managers invest primarily in short-term securities that are nontaxable, such as municipal bonds, etc.

Index

If you took the ideas presented in this book seriously and would like information on upcoming seminars and learning materials and/or would like to learn how to access complimentary financial planning programs, please write, call, or return the coupon below.

BARNHART GROUP

3523 McKinney Avenue,
Dallas, Texas 75204
800/301-3001

Name _____
Address _____
State _____ Zip Code _____
Phone _____ / _____
Fax _____ / _____
Email _____